MAKII
CRAFT (

A CIDERIST'S GUIDE

Simon McKie

SHIRE PUBLICATIONS

DEDICATION

To Sharon,
The good thing that I found, my helpmeet, my glory and my crown.

Published in Great Britain in 2015 by Shire Publications Ltd,
PO Box 883, Oxford OX1 9PL, United Kingdom.
PO Box 3985, New York, NY 10185-3983, USA.
E-mail: shire@shirebooks.co.uk   www.shirebooks.co.uk

© 2011 Simon McKie.
First published 2011; reprinted 2012, 2013, 2014 and 2015.

A CIP catalogue record for this book is available from the British Library.

Shire LIbrary no. 618.   ISBN-13: 978 0 74780 817 6

Simon McKie has asserted his right under the Copyright, Designs and Patents Act, 1988, to be identified as the author of this book.

Designed by Tony Truscott Designs, Sussex, UK
Typeset in Perpetua and Gill Sans.
Printed in China through World Print Ltd.

15 16 17 18 19   14 13 12 11 10 9 8 7 6 5

COVER IMAGES
Cover design and photography by Peter Ashley.

TITLE PAGE IMAGE
Cider: 'a drink made from the juice of apples … expressed and fermented.'

Shire Publications is supporting the Woodland Trust, the UK's leading woodland conservation charity, by funding the dedication of trees.

CONTENTS

ACKNOWLEDGEMENTS

In writing, and selecting the illustrations for, this book I have received generous help from many people. I am grateful to them all and, in making these acknowledgements of their help, I apologise to any whom I may have overlooked. They have contributed greatly to this book and improved it in many ways but the responsibility for any errors that may remain is, of course, entirely mine.

First, I must thank my publishers Shire Publications Ltd and, in particular, Nick Wright, Russell Butcher, Elizabeth Crawford and Emily Brand for their help and encouragement.

I must also acknowledge the considerable help which I have received in identifying suitable illustrations and express my thanks for being permitted to publish them. In particular, I should like to thank The Museum of London (page 13 top), the Royal Collection (page 12 bottom), the National Portrait Gallery (page 13 bottom), Margaret Thomson and Irene Orchard of the Cider Museum of Hereford and H. P. Bulmer (pages 30 top, and 31), Neil Phillips – www.orchardeye.com – (page 1), Vicky Gorman of Fruit Shark (page 39 top right), Jez Howatt of the Cider Workshop (page 8 bottom), Simon Russell and Dafne Alonso of the National Association of Cidermakers (pages 14 top and bottom, 19 top left, 24 bottom, and 32 top left), Claude Jollicoeur (page 76), Julian Temperley of the Somersetshire Cider Brandy Company Ltd (page 81), and Michael Richardson, Hannah Lowery and Jamie Carstairs of the University of Bristol Library Special Collections (pages 15 top and bottom, 16, 17 top and bottom, and 83). I am especially grateful to Camilla Bridewell of Vigo Ltd (pages 38 top, 40 top and bottom, 43 all, 54 bottom, 55, 57, 58, 63 top left, 65 bottom, 74 top and bottom, and 80) and David Walker of the Somersetshire Rural Life Museum (pages 34, 41 top and bottom, 42 all, and 84) who were particularly generous with their time, help and advice.

I would also like to thank Martin Haswell of MHDI Ltd for his professionalism, creativity and care in taking the photographs of our cidermaking with family and friends here at Rudge Hill House.

In writing Chapter 7, I have benefited from the advice of Her Majesty's Revenue and Customs and of Mendip District Council and I am grateful to the individuals in those bodies who took time to answer my questions. My discussion, however, of the licensing of the sale and supply of alcohol, food hygiene regulations and Excise Duties in Chapter 7 expresses my understanding of the law and is not necessarily the opinion of those bodies.

Craft cidermakers are an enthusiastic and kindly bunch. A glance at the leading cider forum, the Cider Workshop (www.ciderworkshop.com), reveals an online community, the members of which are unfailingly courteous and generous in sharing their information, advice and experience. I owe a debt of gratitude to all who have contributed to that forum.

Three of the most prolific and generous contributors to the Cider Workshop forum, Nick Edwards, Jez Howat and Andrew Lea, undertook the onerous task of reading this book in draft. They bear no responsibility for any errors it may contain but their suggestions have enormously improved it. I am very grateful to them.

It would be impractical to list all of the authors whose works I have found useful. A selection is given in Appendix 5. I have found, for example, the works listed there by James Crowden, Joan Morgan and Alison Richards and R. K. French of great help in composing the historical summary in Chapter 1. I must, however, record my debt to Andrew Lea. In his own book on craft cidermaking, in his contributions to cider fora and in many other ways he has taught, with patience and tact, a whole generation of ciderists, including myself, the essentials of the craft, solved their difficulties and answered their questions. In this book I have tried to share the fruits of my experience of making cider. In common with many others, much of what I know has been learnt from Andrew's writings and this book reflects that fact in every chapter.

Cidermaking is mostly learnt from practical experience. It can be hard physical work but it is an enjoyable and convivial activity. I have had the pleasure of receiving help from many people over the years. In particular, I would like to thank Roger and Vicky Allen, Gillian Arthur, Richard and Cheryl Gould, Sam Hampson, Watty and Tatum Hepburne-Scott, Christopher and Joyce Horley, Jolanda Nowicka, Carrie and J. Pakenham, Nicholas Wilcox, my niece Jasmine Stevens, who has added glamour to our photographs, and my daughters, Letitia and Julia MᶜKie. I am grateful to them all for their contribution to making, and drinking, Rudge Hill Cider.

I would also like to remember with affection and gratitude the help of my late neighbour and good friend, Bryan Stanley, whose practical expertise helped me to solve many of the problems posed in adapting the equipment of a private house and garden for use in cidermaking.

I am very grateful to my personal assistant, Jessica Weeks, for much of the research which identified suitable illustrations for this book and for her help in myriad other ways. In particular, she and Cheryl Gould have shown truly Christian patience in typing the manuscript and its many revisions.

Finally, I owe a debt of gratitude to my wife, Sharon, for reading the manuscript in draft, for making many useful and practical suggestions and for her help with cidermaking over the years. Most of all, I am grateful for her patience and kindness in indulging my hobby and for listening to my conversation which, while I have been writing this book, has had only one topic – cider!

Simon MᶜKie
Rudge Hill House
Rudge
Somersetshire

August 2010

1: CIDERMAKING – TRADITIONAL AND SCIENTIFIC

THE REVIVAL OF CRAFT CIDERMAKING

It appears that cider has been made in Britain since before the Romans came. Since then, as we shall see, its fortunes have waxed and waned but by the end of the twentieth century British cidermaking seemed to have declined to a very low point. Cider, which had once been the pride of the English gentleman's table and the solace of the poor, had come down in the world. On the one hand, 'scrumpy' was made by a dwindling number of artisan makers, mainly in the West Country, whose products were often acetic, cloudy with yeast and a challenge, rather than a pleasure, to drink. On the other hand, there was the mass-produced cider made by the giants of the cider industry, designed to sell on price rather than quality – a light and fruity drink it is true, but with only a minimal apple juice content, and that usually mediated through apple concentrate, with much of its alcohol derived from glucose and artificially sweetened and carbonated. Craft cidermakers often refer to these mass-produced ciders, disparagingly, as 'glucose wine'. I have adopted the term 'industrial cider' in this book as descriptive of the processes by which they are made.

There is, of course, nothing at all wrong with enjoying a simple, refreshing drink at an affordable price or with relishing the straightforward, appley pleasure offered by the better scrumpy. Nonetheless, the eclipse of high-quality or 'fine' cider, a drink that can have a depth and complexity of flavour at least to rival good wine, is, as I and many enthusiasts believe, regrettable.

THE REASONS FOR REVIVAL

Since the mid-1990s the situation has been transformed by three factors. First, there has been a general revival of interest in good food and good drink and, developing from this, an increased interest in what food and drink contains and the methods by which it is made. Second, the internet has allowed enthusiasts in different areas to locate one another and to share their knowledge and enthusiasm. Ironically, however, the single most important

Opposite: Cider has many styles. In the jug we see the darker, more tannic cider of the West Country.

factor in reviving the fortunes of good-quality cidermaking has been the success of the large industrial cider companies in marketing their products. Magners' advertising campaigns, starting in 2003, transformed the public's view of cider. From being seen as an old-fashioned drink drunk only by the old or alcoholic it is now regarded as a refreshing drink for the young. Of the millions who were introduced to industrial cider in this way, some went on to be interested in, and appreciative of, fine cider. They are still only a very small proportion of the total market for cider in this country but they have been sufficient to create a demand that has enabled small commercial cidermakers seriously interested in creating fine cider to flourish.

It has also had another beneficial effect: it has stimulated the desire of an increasing minority to make fine cider for consumption

Cider has a complexity of flavour to rival that of wine.

Google Groups
Subscribe to the Cider Workshop
Email: [   ] [Subscribe]
Visit the Cider Workshop group

The Cider Workshop

Home | Production | Pomona | Orchards | Events | Links | Scrattings | Archive | Blogs

Welcome to ciderworkshop.com, the web resource for the Cider Workshop Google group - the friendly community of craft cider & perry makers and enthusiasts.

Anyone can join the **Cider Workshop discussion group** and ask questions or simply discuss real cider and perry (or as some of us prefer, craft cider and perry - there is no real difference). The **cider workshop.com** web resource is an easy reference for all cider lovers and as a storage space of ideas and expertise for the group.

The group discuss all aspects of growing, making and consuming cider (and Perry, Calvados, Pommeau etc.) from orchard to glass. This includes stuff as varied as travel, poetry, advertising, marketing, legal aspects and story telling, as well as methods, equipment and reviews. See the Cider Workshop mission statement below.

Cider making is a broad church, and comes with many different practices and opinions. Although the Cider Workshop is primarily a UK cider and perry group, there are a number of members from the USA, as well as Europe and Australia. So, if cider and perry are of interest to you please join us in the discussion group. And if you have any ideas that would be good to capture in the website, please do let us know!

Search the Cider Workshop
[Google Custom Search] [Search]

How to make cider
The Workshop outlets map
Cider Workshop resources

The Cider Workshop website – an invaluable source of information, advice and shared experience.

The Cider Workshop - a safe place for intoxicating debate!

Whats happening in the cider workshop?		
Updates	Scrattings	Events
• Commercial - added planning	• Clearing a standard tree	• TCCPA 2010 results

It is a pleasure to make cider to be enjoyed and savoured by family and friends.

by themselves and their family and friends. It is this group to which I belong and to whom this book is addressed. In it I attempt to distil and share the knowledge which I have acquired through my own cidermaking, taking the reader through the whole process of cidermaking from the selection of apple varieties to drinking the finished product. I hope that those considering starting cidermaking will find in this book the information they need to enable them to do so and that even experienced cidermakers may find in it something of value.

TERMINOLOGY

My subject is cidermaking, the aim of which is to make, not the highest quantity of cider for the lowest possible cost in money or time, but rather the highest-quality cider that is practicable. Those who have that aim have suggested several terms to distinguish their activity from industrial cidermaking on the one hand and the production of poor-quality scrumpy on the other. Some have suggested adopting the old spelling 'cyder' but that, perhaps, suggests too much the bogus archaism of the 'olde tea shoppe' and ignores the large amount of modern scientific knowledge that underlies the production of good cider. Others have suggested the term 'real cider' by analogy with the Campaign for Real Ale. The term that is gaining acceptance by use, however, is 'craft cider' and that is the term adopted in this book.

The gentlemen of the late seventeenth and early eighteenth centuries whose writings did so much to improve the quality of cider in that period referred to the cidermaker whose concern was to produce fine cider as the 'cyderist' (see for example the *Compleat Planter and Cyderist* published in 1685 and written anonymously by 'A Lover of Planting'). In a modernised spelling, this is the term I have adopted for the craft cidermaker.

WHAT IS CRAFT CIDER?

Many ciderists would say that the term 'craft cider' should be applied only to cider which is made entirely from pressed apple juice and nothing else, and which is fermented from yeasts occurring naturally. It is certainly true that much good cider is made by that method, as well as some that is almost undrinkable. The process of making cider, however, is not one which easily occurs in nature. The accidental fermentation of juice will not produce any significant volume of drinkable cider. It is only in the artificially constructed environment of the fermenting vessel that conditions are created which are perfect for the reproduction of those yeasts which produce drinkable cider. Ironically, the main strains of yeast which do so, the *saccharomyces*, are present primarily in the general cidermaking environment and not in the apple.

So, I prefer to see the essence of craft cidermaking in the pursuit of quality rather than in 'purity' of ingredients. Nonetheless, cider is, as the *Shorter Oxford English Dictionary* defines it, 'a drink made from the juice of apples … expressed and fermented'. So few ciderists would consider that craft cider could be made with anything other than pressed apple juice overwhelmingly forming the major ingredient. Quite arbitrarily, many would say that craft cider must be made with at least 85 per cent apple juice. Having

Apple juice, the basis of fine cider.

made that proviso, however, many, but not all, ciderists are willing to allow the addition of sugar and the juice of pears, the use of metabisulphite as a sterilising agent, of pectinase, of commercially cultured yeasts and, even, of artificial sweeteners. The advantages and disadvantages of doing so are discussed later in this book.

QUANTITY

As I have said, this book is addressed to the ciderist who makes cider for himself, his family, his friends and neighbours; the 'domestic ciderist'. Such a man (or woman) may make only a few demijohns a year or he may make very much more than that. However large his family may be and however generous he may be to his friends and relatives, the domestic ciderist is unlikely to make more than a thousand litres a year, so that is the largest level of production which I consider in this book.

GEOGRAPHICAL AREAS AND STYLES

As we shall see, cider apples are defined by their having been recognised as being peculiarly suitable for cidermaking; but if they have a single feature that distinguishes them from culinary and table apples more than any other, it is their high tannin content (see Chapter 2). The traditional cidermaking areas of England have been in the West Country and in the three counties of Herefordshire, Worcestershire and Gloucestershire; those of Wales have been in the ancient counties of Monmouthshire, Breconshire and Radnorshire. In these counties, the cider has the full body and complex flavours which one associates with tannic fruit. In the eastern counties, however, and elsewhere in England and Wales, cider is often made from culinary and table apples.

Writing in *The Listener* on 7 October 1931, P. Morton Shand explained the geographical variations in styles of cider:

> In Herefordshire and North of the Severn generally, the cider is light and brisk, though the best is nutty and mellow. Devonshire cider is heavier and sweeter and often luscious as honey. In Worcestershire it is light yellow in colour and has a tart and stimulating aftertaste. Somersetshire cider is more of the Norman type, full of flavour, but with a pronounced acid tang. Excellent cider is now made in Kent, but it lacks a characteristic savour. Norfolk cider is dark and rather flat and insipid.

The cidermakers of Norfolk and Kent might not have agreed with this characterisation of their products but it is true that outside the traditional cider areas, the cider made is lighter and less tannic. Its detractors say that it is less complex and interesting than the cider from the main traditional cidermaking areas, but many like it for its freshness and lightness of taste.

Like wine, there are many different styles of cider and an appreciation of one need not preclude an appreciation of another. Today's ciderists are developing a wide range of styles of cider dependent upon *terroir*, cultivar, sweetness, conditioning, age and storage vessel. In doing so they are simply recovering the forgotten expertise of their predecessors.

A LITTLE HISTORY

THE MEDIEVAL AND TUDOR PERIODS

By the late Middle Ages, cider was a national drink. Even in West Sussex, which nobody would now think of as a prime cidermaking area, in 1341, seventy-four of the eighty parishes paid tithes in cider. In the thirteenth century, Giraldus Cambrensis remarked, as evidence of their luxurious tastes, on the preference of the monks of Canterbury for cider over Kentish ale. Most monasteries planted orchards of at least 3 acres to provide cider for their own consumption and for sale at a profit. By the later Middle Ages, cider was a drink equal in popularity to ale so that, when the followers of the reformer John Wycliffe came to translate the Bible into English in the fourteenth century, it was natural that they should translate the Hebrew 'shekar' meaning 'strong drink' as 'cyder'.

The style of the eastern counties – light and refreshing.

Cider declined in popularity in the early sixteenth century when the brewing of ale was transformed into the brewing of beer by the new practice of adding hops, improving both its keeping quality and its taste.

THE ROOTS OF REVIVAL IN THE SEVENTEENTH CENTURY

The rise of Puritanism and the religious controversies of the first half of the seventeenth century began cider's revival in popular esteem. The Puritans prized cidermaking as part of a regimen of self-sufficiency and industry giving a prelapsarian dominion over nature. Cider's prestige travelled with the Pilgrim Fathers to North America where it remained high until the temperance movement changed the continent's relationship with alcohol.

It wasn't just the Puritans who valued cidermaking. John Beale (1608–1683), the Vicar of Yeovil, records Charles I's preference for cider during the Great Rebellion:

When the late King (of blessed memory) came to Herefordshire, in his distress, and such of the gentry of Worcestershire as were brought thither as prisoners; both King, Nobility and Gentry, did prefer … [cider] … before the best wines those parts afforded.

THE LONG EIGHTEENTH CENTURY: A GOLDEN AGE OF CIDERMAKING

It is with the Restoration, however, that the pre-eminence of cider, which was to continue throughout the eighteenth century, began. The agricultural depression of the 1660s stimulated farmers and landowners to search for supplemental sources of income and the Royal Society was a focus for efforts to improve agriculture by the application of scientific knowledge. It was the time of the publication of a number of important works on cidermaking including John Evelyn's *Sylva*, published in 1664. This included an Addendum, *A Pomona*, on the cultivation of cider orchards and the making of cider to which John Beale contributed. John Worlidge (1640–1700) wrote *Vinetum Britannicum or A Treatise of Cider* which was published in 1676, and John Phillips (1676–1709) wrote an entire poem (of 1,500 lines) on the subject of cider, *Cyder: A Poem*, which was first published in 1708.

As we shall see, the traditional way of making sparkling alcoholic drinks is either to bottle them when there is still some unfermented residual sugar in the cider or by adding a little additional sugar on bottling to a fully fermented liquid. The result is that fermentation continues in the bottle, carbon dioxide is released and, being under pressure, is absorbed into the liquid. When the bottle's closure is removed, the pressure is released and carbon dioxide escapes from the liquid in the form of bubbles. Ciderists refer

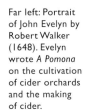

Opposite bottom: Portrait of Charles I by Sir Anthony Van Dyck (1633). John Beale recorded the Martyr King's preference for cider over wine.

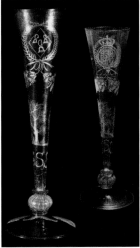

Far left: Portrait of John Evelyn by Robert Walker (1648). Evelyn wrote *A Pomona* on the cultivation of cider orchards and the making of cider.

Left: A fine cider flute made in 1650 for Viscount Scudamore, formerly British Ambassador to France, a keen ciderist and promoter and improver of cider manufacture.

13

An eighteenth-century cider glass. Fine cider was the pride of the eighteenth-century gentleman's table.

to this as 'bottle conditioning'. It is the basis of the *méthode champenoise* used in making champagne and other quality sparkling wines.

Thomas Stevenson (in the 1998 *Christie's World Encyclopaedia of Champagne and Sparkling Wine*) and James Crowden have unearthed a body of evidence which demonstrates that bottle conditioning was first developed and commercially applied in England in the middle of the seventeenth century. Perhaps it might be more appropriate to call the *méthode champenoise* the 'English method'.

Throughout the eighteenth century, cider grew in popularity. Two distinct markets developed. The first was for ordinary cider, drunk by working men and women as an alternative to beer and with an alcoholic strength of 4 or 5 per cent. Often it was made by soaking already pressed must in water and pressing it a second time. The resulting drink was known as 'small cider', 'ciderkin' or, simply, as 'beverage'. The second market was for fine cider drunk by gentlemen as an alternative to foreign wine. The two types of cider sold at widely differing prices. Price information cited by R. K. French in *The History and Virtues of Cyder* suggests that in 1794 fine cider might have had a market value more than forty times that of the ordinary cider given to agricultural workers as part of their wages; a common practice in the cidermaking counties. The *English Encyclopaedia*, published in 1859, recorded that at harvest time agricultural labourers would drink as much as twenty-four pints of cider during a working day although the usual allowance was two quarts per day for a man and one quart for a boy. The practice of paying wages with cider was made illegal by the Cider Truck Act (1887) but advertisements offering farmworkers 'good house and cider' were still appearing in Somersetshire newspapers in the 1940s.

Agricultural workers' wages were paid partly in cider until the Cider Truck Act (1887) made the practice illegal.

Patriotism and economics combined to increase cider's prestige. For gentlemen to consume fine cider rather than foreign wines was seen as reducing the country's dependence upon foreign imports and retaining English currency within the country. Because brewing beer requires the application of heat during the processes of malting and mashing and of boiling the wort, it was thought good that working men should drink cider rather than beer so as to reduce the nation's consumption of wood, which was considered to be important for the maintenance of the Navy.

The Napoleonic Wars further confirmed cider's status as a gentleman's drink because imports of wine from France, her dependent territories and allies were not available. By then, however, other economic factors were already undermining cider's status.

DECLINE IN THE NINETEENTH CENTURY

In the 1760s a condition associated with the working men of Devonshire known as 'the cyder colic' was found to be simple lead poisoning caused by the use of lead in the various processes of manufacturing cider in Devonshire. Cider's reputation as a healthy drink was lowered and the outbreak began the identification in the public mind of cider as a working man's drink. The ending of the Napoleonic Wars meant that rich men could once again import wine. Its novelty made it fashionable so that gentlemen competed in serving foreign wines rather than fine cider at their tables. Once gentlemen had ceased to drink cider it came to be regarded as the drink of the lower classes. The market for fine cider disappeared and only low-quality bulk production was economically viable. The existence of a large-scale market in ordinary cider coupled with the decline of the market for fine cider led to a decline in the standards of cidermaking and the exclusive pursuit of low prices rather than quality.

A BRIEF REVIVAL

Towards the end of the nineteenth century cidermaking was at a low point. It was partially revived by a number of enthusiasts giving rise to a new research activity – resulting in the publication, for example, of *Apples and Pears as Vintage Fruits*

Sir Robert Neville (1846–1936), the founder of the research laboratory that developed into the Long Ashton Research Station, outside the cider house at Butleigh Court, c. 1930.

Butleigh Court, where Sir Robert Neville set up his laboratories.

by Dr R. Hogg and Dr H. G. Bull in 1886, which listed the best cider and pear varieties including the details of their average specific gravities. In 1893 Sir Robert Neville set up laboratories at his home at Butleigh Court near Glastonbury, which in due course attracted government support and led to the setting up of the National Fruit and Cider Institute in 1903 in the village of Long Ashton outside Bristol. The Institute made a collection of cider apple and perry pear fruits and evaluated them, applying the latest biological and biochemical developments to cider production. The Institute became part of the University of Bristol in 1912, changing its name to the Long Ashton Research Station. The station ceased its work on fruit and cider in 1985, concentrating on work in respect of arable crops, and was finally closed in 2003.

TWENTIETH- AND TWENTY-FIRST-CENTURY DECLINE AND REVIVAL

In the twentieth century, cider continued to suffer from its reputation as a poor man's drink. The growth of industrial cider production drove the small producers out of the market and resulted in the creation of a uniform low-price product, much as happened in the beer market before the resurgence of interest in real ale.

As we have seen, however, at the end of the last century and the beginning of the new one there was a great revival of interest in the production of craft cider among both commercial and domestic ciderists.

The Butleigh
Court Cider Team,
c. 1895.

COMPARATIVE TASTING

The ciderist's aim is to make good-quality cider. How is one to define and describe such cider? The ciderist knows from experience that cider can be as subtle and complex a drink as wine. Winemakers and wine connoisseurs have developed over centuries a specialised descriptive vocabulary to isolate and describe the different sensory experiences that make up the experience of drinking wine and to describe the variations within them. Ciderists and other

The main building of the Long Ashton Research Station in 1928.

The cider building at Long Ashton Research Station.

cider connoisseurs have not done so to anything like the same extent. Experienced ciderists do, however, develop a palate that can exactly discriminate between good and bad cider, making use of a vocabulary mainly drawn from the appreciation of wine. In order to aim at a target one must know what it is, and so the ciderist needs to spend some time tasting ciders from a wide variety of producers so as to develop his palate to appreciate the differences between the good and the bad, and between different styles. He also needs to determine what processes affect the taste, colour and aroma of his final product.

EXPERIMENTATION AND RECORDING

The chemical changes that occur in fruit juice during the processes of fermentation and maturation are extremely complex. The relationships between what goes into the must and what happens to it during those processes on the one hand, and the flavour of the resulting cider (or wine) on the other, is not straightforward. Experimentation and recording are the key to successful cidermaking. Experimentation involves making carefully planned variations from one's normal processes so as to see the effects of the variation on the resulting cider. Unless one has a photographic and permanent memory, recording is necessary to enable one to build up a body of experience based on those variations. What is more, one cannot make variations from a norm until a norm is established. The new ciderist, therefore, needs to have a basic method of operation that can be relied on to produce good-quality cider, which he can fine-tune once he has acquired the necessary experience.

AN ESSENTIALLY SIMPLE PROCESS

In the chapters and appendices that follow I try to provide the new ciderist with that basic method and to suggest changes which might be made to it and solutions to common problems. In order to be comprehensive, it has been necessary for me to go into some detail. In its essentials, however, cidermaking is really quite straightforward. It is a natural process directed by science. A cidermaker who simply presses apples and allows the juice to ferment and mature in appropriate vessels will, provided he is scrupulous in cleaning and sterilising his equipment, usually find that the cider he makes is of a quality higher than that of industrial cider and that it will satisfy the discerning palate and soothe the weary spirit.

2: APPLE SELECTION AND HARVESTING

Of course, the starting point of cidermaking is the selection of apples.

PROPAGATION

In nature trees propagate by growing from seed. Trees which have propagated in this way are called 'seedlings'. Where they have grown by accident rather than deliberate planting they are also called 'wildings'. Where, as is the case with most apple trees, they cannot self-pollinate, the resulting tree will combine the DNA of the pollinated tree and that of the tree from which the pollen has come. Except in carefully controlled experimental conditions, it is impractical to attempt to control the pollen that falls on a tree. Even where, in controlled experiments, trees are pollinated by identified pollen, trees grown from the resulting apple seeds show large degrees of variation from the parent trees and from each other. So one cannot propagate seedlings reliably to produce predictable variations in characteristics as one does in breeding farm and domestic animals by combining males and females with complementary characteristics.

Above left: Cider in the making.

Above: This wilding has probably grown from an apple core from an orchard nearby, dropped by a deer.

The blossom gives promise of the apples to come...

...and is beautiful in itself.

Apples trees may be propagated asexually by grafting a cutting (or scion) onto another young tree (the rootstock). When the graft grows it has only the DNA of the tree from which the scion has been cut; it is a clone. The original tree's DNA may be cloned many times in this way to form a single variety. Such varieties are known as cultivars. Of course, it is possible to take any seedling, cultivate it until it bears fruit and then determine the characteristics of its fruit. If it has good characteristics one can then propagate it repeatedly by grafting, so defining a new cultivar; that is, indeed, how new apple cultivars are developed.

Bees carry pollen from tree to tree.

Using apples from identifiable cultivars allows one to use fruit with reasonably predictable qualities. Those qualities will still vary, however, from tree to tree, from apple to apple and from year to year.

Above left: Young cider apple trees. In the foreground is a tree of the Nehou cultivar.

THE KEY QUALITIES
The most important qualities of apples which the ciderist needs to consider are their sugar, acid and tannin content and, beyond these three, their 'flavour', which is very much more difficult to define and measure.

Above: A young cider apple tree of the Broxwood Foxwhelp cultivar in blossom.

SUGAR CONTENT
In fermentation, yeasts convert sugar into ethyl alcohol (also referred to as ethanol) and carbon dioxide. It is because of the release of carbon dioxide that bubbles rise to the surface in a fermenting liquid. Because a given quantity of alcohol will be produced by a given quantity of sugar, if the liquid is fermented to dryness its potential alcohol content will be determined by its sugar content. We shall see in the next chapter how to measure sugar content. The sugar content of the apples, therefore, will, unless other sources of sugar are added to the mix, determine the potential alcohol content of the final product.

ACIDITY
The natural acid contained in apples is 90 per cent malic acid, and 10 per cent quinic acid. The acidity of the must (that is the juice) from which the cider

21

is made is of importance for two reasons. First, it inhibits the development of microbial infection; and second, it affects flavour. A must with too little acid will produce a cider which tastes flaccid and dull. One with too much acid will be tart. As we shall see there are two methods of measuring acidity. The first is to measure pH, the value of which correlates closely with the prevention of microbial infection. The second is to measure total acidity through titration. The value of total acid correlates closely to the perception of acidity by taste. The pH value and total acidity correlate loosely, but not exactly, with one another.

TANNINS

Tannins are a diverse and complex group of plant polyphenols, which occur in many fruits including apples. Tannin has a bitter and astringent taste. When one eats a highly tannic apple, one experiences a feeling of dryness in the mouth which makes the mouth 'pucker'. Tannin is described as 'soft' if it is bitter but not greatly astringent, and as 'hard' if it is both bitter and strongly astringent. In most fruits, substantial amounts of tannin are only found in the pips, stalks and skins but apples are an exception to this and high levels of tannin are found in the flesh of crab apples and in that of most of the cultivars that have been selected as particularly suitable for cidermaking over the years. In the process of fermentation and maturation, chemical changes occur which 'soften' the flavours resulting from the presence of tannins, reducing the bitterness and astringency of the cider and increasing its complexity and depth of flavour. The determination of the tannin content of a juice by analysis is an expert process not easily performed without scientific training. It is usual, therefore, for the domestic ciderist to determine the tannin content by taste rather than analysis.

The Long Ashton Research Station developed a standard classification of cider apples into four categories depending upon their acid and tannin contents. The classification is as follows:

	Bittersweet percentage	Bittersharp percentage	Sweet percentage	Sharp percentage
Acid	≤0.45	>0.45	≤0.45	>0.45
Tannin	>0.20	>0.20	≤0.20	≤0.20

It will be seen that the difference between bittersweet and sweet cider apples on the one hand and bittersharp and sharp cider apples on the other is not their sugar content, but their acidity. Bittersharps and bittersweets are further divided into mild, medium and full according to their tannin content.

CRAB APPLES

Whereas the great majority of cultivated apples belong to the species *malus domestica*, a descendant of *malus pumila* which seems to have originated in Khirgizia, the true English crab apple belongs to the species *malus sylvestris*.

True crab apples tend to be high in tannin and can be used in small proportions as a useful source of tannin where cider is being made primarily from table and culinary apples. Care is needed, however, because many apples called crabs are in fact wildings resulting from the pips of cultivated apples. The best way of telling whether a supposed crab apple is suitable for blending is to taste it to see if it has the characteristic bitter and astringent taste of hard tannin.

DETERMINING THE SOURCES FROM WHICH TO OBTAIN ONE'S APPLES

Culinary apples are marked by high acidity and, often, by low sugar levels. Table apples tend to have low acidity and high sugar levels. Both culinary and table apples have low tannin content. The acidity of table apples, however, is not necessarily less than that of a sharp or bittersharp cider apple. The secret of successful cidermaking is to achieve a blend in which the proportions of tannins and acid are correct and in which the sugar content will result in the desired percentage of alcohol in the final cider. As we shall see, that blending is best done after pressing and immediately before the start of fermentation with adjustments made at the end of fermentation. In determining the sources from which to obtain one's apples, however, it is important to have regard to their characteristics so that one can have suitable apple juice available to create a must with the required characteristics. It is highly unlikely that one could achieve that with a single cultivar. Some commercial cidermakers sell single-varietal ciders just as single-varietal wines are sold. As with wine, such single-varietal ciders will often contain a small proportion of other cultivars to produce the necessary balance.

BALANCING SUGAR, ACIDITY AND TANNIN

Many ciderists would say that the ideal level of acid and tannin in the must is 0.4 per cent of total acid and 0.2 per cent of tannin although there will be a range of views over the tannin content. In order to prevent bacterial infection, the pH of the juice should be in the range 3.2–3.8. Sugar content should not be less than 10 per cent, which, if the must is fermented to dryness, will give a final alcohol content of about 6 per cent by volume. Most ciderists would

A careful
determination
of flavour.

want a considerably higher alcohol content than
that. A typical bittersweet cider apple might
have a sugar content of as much as 15 per cent
whereas the sugar content of a culinary apple
might be 8 per cent or even lower.

FLAVOUR

Even if one has created a blend which balances
acidity and tannin and has the required sugar
content, one still has to consider the more
amorphous quality of flavour. There is no simple
relationship between the flavour of an apple and
the resulting flavour of the cider.

Cider apples are not defined solely by their acid and tannin content. They
are simply apples from those cultivars which have been recognised as suitable
for cidermaking over the years. 'Suitability' has been determined by practice
and experience and a consensus has emerged among ciderists as to which
cultivars are most suitable. The criteria for selection will not have been
confined to flavour. Resistance to disease, storage life and ease of pressing,
for example, will all have influenced the recognition of a cultivar as suitable
for cidermaking. The flavour of the resulting cider, however, will have been
of primary importance.

Within the class of cider apples certain apples have been recognised as
being suitable for producing 'vintage-quality' cider. There is not a complete

Harry Master's
Jersey apples. This
cultivar is a
vintage-quality
medium
bittersweet from
Somersetshire.

Classification	Degree	Cultivar
Bittersweet	Mild	Sercombes Natural, Somersetshire Redstreak
	Medium	Harry Master's Jersey, Yarlington Mill
	Full	Ashton Brown Jersey, Dabinett, Major, Medaille D'Or
Bittersharp	Mild	Kingston Black
	Medium	Broxwood Foxwhelp, Dymock Red, Stoke Red
	Full	Cap of Liberty
Sweet		Court Royal, Northwood, Sweet Coppin
Sharp		Brown's Apple, Backwell Red, Crimson King, Fair Maid of Devon, Frederick

consensus as to which cultivars are of vintage quality but the following is a list of some which are generally accepted to be so. The apples to which the description 'vintage quality' has been given are those which are most suitable to making cider in the style of the traditional cidermaking areas. Even among ciderists, however, there is a developing taste for a lighter style of cider which mixes culinary and table apples with cider apples.

BALANCING SOURCES OF APPLES OF DIFFERENT CULTIVARS

If land is available for the purpose, one can plant trees specifically for cidermaking. If that is not possible or while one waits for the trees one has planted to grow, one can make cider from whatever apples are available. There are many people who have apple trees in their gardens who have a surplus of apples. One will often find that family, neighbours and friends are happy to allow one to take produce which would otherwise go to waste. Similarly, wildings may be found growing on the roadside or on common land. Roadside trees are often the result of apple cores thrown from cars. One must be careful to test the juice from such trees to determine its qualities before using them in cider production.

It may also be important to accept that, in order to achieve the right balance, one must not use all of the fruit which is available. If for example one has a reasonable quantity of table apples and a much larger quantity of culinary apples, in order to achieve a balance one might decide to use only some of the culinary apples in order to avoid making a juice which is overly acidic.

Some years ago, on moving house, I acquired land with ten apple trees: three table, six culinary and one crab apple tree. I planted one tree each of the following cultivars, opting for a preponderance of bittersweets so as to balance my existing trees:

- Nehou (a full bittersweet)
- Dymock Red
- Broxwood Foxwhelp
- Harry Master's Jersey
- Somersetshire Redstreak
- Major
- Stoke Red
- Dabinett
- Ashton Brown Jersey
- Pigsnout (a sweet cider apple)
- Fair Maid of Devon
- Kingston Black

They are bearing fruit now but, until they did, I made what I consider to be excellent cider in the eastern style entirely from culinary and table apples from my own trees and from those of my friends and neighbours.

IDENTIFYING THE CULTIVAR OF AN APPLE

When one has acquired mature apple trees on the purchase of a property or when one presses apples donated by others, the variety of the apples concerned may not be known. There are many interesting apple trees, knowledge of the identity of the cultivar of which has been lost. Of course, the acidity and sugar content of the juice from the apple can be easily determined and an assessment made of its tannin content from taste. Without knowing the type of apple, however, it will be difficult to predict the flavour characteristics which the pressed juice will impart to one's cider. The cultivar of an apple is identified by its characteristics: when the tree from which it came pollinates, when the apples from that tree ripen and fall and the apple's botanic features, including the colour of its skin, its size and shape and the nature of its eye, basin, cavity and stalk, and the colour, texture and flavour of its flesh.

The New Book of Apples by Joan Morgan and Alison Richards provides a directory of apples described by reference to these characteristics and *A Somersetshire Pomona* by Liz Copas provides a directory with descriptions and very useful photographs of Somersetshire cider apples. In addition, the National Fruit Collection at Brogdale provides an efficient and inexpensive apple identification service.

Seedlings, of course, cannot be identified with an existing cultivar because their DNA will be a unique combination of the DNA of the pollinating and pollinated trees.

TERROIR AND ORCHARD MANAGEMENT

In cider production, as in wine production, opinions differ greatly as to the importance of *terroir* – that is, the complete natural environment in which the cider or wine is produced, including such factors as soil, typography and climate. Difficult though it is to define their effect, differences in the natural environment in which apples of a cultivar are grown do lead to differences in the flavour of those apples and of the cider produced from them. In his book *Ciderland*, James Crowden records that the Long Ashton Research Station recognised three areas of Somersetshire as being areas in which vintage-quality cider was produced. Those were Kingsbury Episcopi, Baltonsborough and Wedmore. The domestic ciderist does not need to define the precise relationship between flavour and *terroir* for, if it is correct to say that *terroir* is important in determining the quality of apples, its effect will show in the qualities of the apples produced from any particular location.

The way in which an orchard is prepared and managed will affect very significantly the quality of the apples which are produced. Orchard management is outside the scope of a book of this size but is an essential skill for those growing their own apples for cider production.

PEARS AS AN INGREDIENT IN CIDER

Apples, pears, medlars and quinces are all pomes belonging to the same sub-family – the *Maloideae*. Perry is the fermented juice of pears. Just as, over time, cider apples have been selected for their suitability for the making of cider, so particular pear cultivars, perry pears, have been selected for their suitability for the making of perry. Pear juice can, however, also be added in small quantities to a cider must, adding a particular quality to it.

Pears contain small quantities of sorbitol, an unfermentable sugar alcohol which has a sweet taste. An average pear is 2 per cent sorbitol. Apples also contain sorbitol but of a lesser amount than pears; the average is about 0.5 per cent. Even when the must is fermented to dryness, therefore, there will be some residual sweetness. Substituting pear juice for apple juice will increase the amount of sorbitol in the fermented cider. The actual increase in the sweetness of the must will not be very much. Sorbitol is 70 per cent as sweet as sucrose. The sweetness arising from sorbitol in pear juice, therefore, is equivalent to a 1.4 per cent solution of sugar and that from apples is equivalent to a 0.35 per cent solution. Assuming that one does not want less than 85 per cent of the must to consist of apple juice, the maximum amount of pear juice in the must would be 15 per cent. Even if one added this maximum amount, the resulting increase in the sweetness of the must would, therefore, only be equivalent to sucrose of 0.16 per cent ((1.40–0.35 per cent) x 0.15 per cent). An off-dry cider has a sugar content of about 1 per cent.

Nonetheless, adding this proportion of pear juice would be sufficient to reduce the perceived dryness of the cider. The addition of pear juice to cider increases the drinker's perception of its sweetness to a rather greater extent than the actual increase in its sweetness because pears are low in acid and so adding pear juice to the must decreases its average acid content. The presence of acid decreases the drinker's perception of sweetness. In addition, the fruit flavours found in pears, which result from natural esters, survive fermentation better than those found in apples. Fruit flavours increase the drinker's perception of sweetness. Taking all of these factors together, the addition of a proportion of pear juice to the must can give a touch of sweetness and fruitiness to an otherwise entirely dry cider.

Sorbitol also has laxative qualities. Fortunately, the addition of pear juice to the must in the small proportions which we have been discussing is unlikely to have any significant laxative effects on a drinker of the resulting cider. There is an odd saying that perry 'goes down like velvet, around like thunder and out like lightning'. Cider with a small addition of pear juice will not be so stormy.

ESTIMATING VOLUME
APPLE YIELD

A ciderist planning to make cider from apples from his own or others' trees will want to know what volume of cider he can expect. Any estimates must be very broad. The yield from a tree will depend upon its size, its age and its general condition and individual qualities and will vary widely from year to year. Some trees are biennial and only bear fruit in alternate years. The size to which a tree will grow is primarily determined by the rootstock on which it is grown. A dwarf tree will grow to a final height of 2–3.5 metres, a semi-dwarf to 3.5–4.5 metres, a half standard to 4.5–6 metres and a standard tree to 6–7.5 metres. The amount of juice in an apple will vary according to its type, size, the way in which its tree has been managed, the amount of rainfall and sunshine in the year in which it is grown, its ripeness when it is harvested and the amount of time between its falling or being picked from the tree and its being pressed.

Remembering that there will be very large variations in yield both between trees of the same size and between years in respect of the same tree, one can say that an average yield might be 30 kg of apples from a fully grown dwarf tree, 100 kg from a semi-dwarf tree, 150 kg from a half standard and 200 kg from a standard tree.

JUICE YIELD

The amount of juice extracted from apples will depend upon the absolute amount of juice in the apple and the efficiency of the press used. Conventionally, the efficiency of a press is expressed as the ratio of the weight

of juice extracted to the weight of apples pressed. So if a press extracts 7 kg of juice from 10 kg of apples it is said to be 70 per cent efficient. In fact, this ratio understates the real efficiency because the apples do not consist entirely of juice so no press will ever be 100 per cent efficient on this measure. As a rough rule of thumb, kilograms of juice extracted can be equated with litres so as to estimate the volume of apple juice one can expect. This will marginally overestimate the potential volume of juice. That is because apple juice is rather denser than water: 1 litre of water weighs 1 kg; 70 kg of juice is likely to have a volume of 66–68 litres, depending upon its sugar content.

These mature apple trees on semi-dwarfing stock are about 4 metres high.

CALCULATING A TYPICAL YIELD

Putting all this information together, therefore, if one has five mature semi-dwarf trees producing 500 kg (5 x 100 kg) of apples, and one uses a rack and cloth press which is 70 per cent efficient, one might hope to produce 350 kg (500 kg x 70 per cent) of apple juice, being 335 litres (350 x 67/70). During the process of fermentation, the must would lose a small amount of volume because of the release of carbon dioxide. A more significant loss of liquid would be due to the process of racking (see Chapter 4) as, on each racking, a small amount of lees and cider are discarded. Losses from these causes should not exceed 10 per cent. If 5 per cent were lost during fermentation and storage, this would give a final volume of cider in our example of 318 litres (335 litres x 95 per cent).

A Herefordshire apple harvest in 1908 – gathering apples can be backbreaking work.

The same harvest in 1908: a satisfying pile.

Bagging the apples in Herefordshire, 1908.

HARVESTING

DETERMINING RIPENESS

As apples ripen, the starches in the apple are converted into sugar and their acid content decreases. They will fall from the tree when they are ripe. Apples for cidermaking, therefore, should not be harvested until the apples are beginning to fall from the tree in some quantity. At that stage the remaining apples on the tree come off easily in the hand without the need for a vigorous tug. If apples are harvested from the tree before they are ready to drop, their sugar will not have been fully developed and they are likely to be too acidic. In the days leading up to the harvesting, one should gather up those apples that have dropped so as to protect them from pest and insect damage.

To tell if the apples on a tree are ripe and ready for harvest, cut an apple open and look at the pips. If the pips are uniformly brown the apple will be ripe. A further test is to place a drop of tincture of iodine on a freshly cut slice of apple. If it immediately becomes purple/black in colour it indicates the presence of starch and therefore that the apple has not yet converted the greater part of its starch into sugar and is not yet fully ripe.

Apples being shaken from young trees in a large orchard.

Bringing in the apples after harvesting.

METHOD

On the day of harvesting one should spread a tarpaulin around each tree in turn and shake the tree so as to bring down the remaining apples. If the apples do not fall easily with shaking, one is harvesting too early. The apples may be bruised in falling from the tree but that will not matter. Rotten apples, however, or apples showing significant insect damage should be discarded. For the quantities required by domestic ciderists, it is unlikely that mechanical methods of picking up the apples will be used. The use of the tarpaulin makes it easier to gather the apples.

DATE OF HARVEST

Apples ripen at different times according to their type, the local climate and variations in the weather conditions in particular years. Apples suitable for cidermaking are unlikely to be ready for harvesting before 1 September and all will usually have been harvested by the end of November.

STORING BEFORE PRESSING

After harvesting, the starch in the apples will continue to be converted into sugar and for this reason it is usual to store the apples for a couple of weeks or even longer.

The apples should be stored in such a way as to protect them from pests. To prevent rot they should be dry and should have a reasonable flow of air around them. So it is best if the apples are left in the sun for a while to dry and are then placed in latticed boxes. It may be possible to obtain plastic fruit trays from a local greengrocer. Failing that, suitable plastic latticed boxes can be purchased (see Appendix 6). Robust plastic storage boxes are expensive but they will last for many years and so they are a sensible capital investment.

Apples need to be stored after the harvest, protected from pests and air must be allowed to circulate around them.

The apples of each cultivar should be kept separate from those of other cultivars so that they can be pressed separately and their characteristics recorded.

Apples with broken skins, or that have extensive bruising, might be pressed on the day of harvesting. They are likely to rot if they are kept for the normal two-week period. Of course, the juice made from these apples will be a little lower in sugar than those made from apples which have been stored.

3: FROM APPLES TO MUST

CLEANING AND STERILISING EQUIPMENT

It is a popular myth that traditional cidermakers show a blithe disregard for cleanliness and hygiene. Cider made in that way is likely to be undrinkable even if it is not dangerous. All equipment that comes into contact with the juice, must or cider should be clean and sterile.

It is important to understand the distinction between cleaning, which is concerned with removing dirt, and sterilising, which involves killing harmful organisms. To clean equipment one should use a non-foaming detergent designed for food equipment use. Regular household detergents should not be used because they are often scented and the suds are difficult to rinse away fully. It is possible to buy combinations of detergent and steriliser which are useful where equipment is heavily soiled: for example a fermentation bin at the end of fermentation. Where that is not the case, it is often better to simply rinse the equipment with plain water, scrub it thoroughly, wash it with sterilising solution and then rinse it thoroughly again with plain water. That is because even detergents designed for food equipment use are often difficult to rinse from equipment and if any traces are left they will taint the cider.

SOLUTIONS OF SODIUM METABISULPHITE

Cidermakers have been using sulphur dioxide to sterilise equipment since at least the seventeenth century and possibly since ancient times. It is now commonly used in the stable form of a salt; usually either potassium or sodium metabisulphite. Sodium metabisulphite is more frequently used. For sterilising equipment it is diluted with ordinary tap-water. Sodium metabisulphite will usually consist of 50 per cent or more of sulphur dioxide. A 10 per cent sodium metabisulphite solution, therefore, will contain 5 per cent or rather more of sulphur dioxide; a 1 per cent solution will contain 0.5 per cent or more. In this book, in referring to percentages of a sterilising solution, I refer to the percentage by weight of sodium metabisulphite mixed with water and not the percentage of sulphur dioxide in solution.

Opposite:
Apple milling,
c. 1930.

In cidermaking, 'cleanliness is, indeed, next to Godliness' (John Wesley's *Sermons on Several Occasions*, 1788).

Where equipment can be soaked in the solution, a 1 per cent solution is sufficiently strong to sterilise it. If the equipment is an awkward shape and therefore cannot be immersed or filled with the solution it will be necessary to wash the equipment with a brush or cloth soaked in it. For washing with a brush or cloth it is better to use a stronger solution, say, 5 per cent.

A 10 per cent sodium metabisulphite solution will keep for several months with little deterioration in a well-stoppered container. Weaker solutions, however, deteriorate much more quickly. A 1 per cent solution should not be kept for more than a few weeks. My normal practice, therefore, is to make a 10 per cent solution and, if a weaker solution is required, to dilute it at the time of use.

I keep the stock solution in a stoppered demijohn. Demijohns usually have a stated capacity of 1 gallon (just under 4.6 litres). Demijohns rarely have a mark to show the 1-gallon level. Sodium metabisulphite is often sold in 500-gram drums. To make an approximate 10 per cent solution, one 500-gram drum of sodium metabisulphite should be added to a demijohn half-filled with water, which should then be topped up with further water as far as possible, while leaving room for the bung, and then stoppered. When sterilising by soaking add nine parts water to one part of the stock solution.

Sodium metabisulphite gives off a strong and unpleasant smell. One should avoid breathing in the fumes or using it in enclosed and unventilated spaces, and be careful not to allow the solution to splash into one's eyes. Having said that, accidentally breathing in fumes or splashing a drop into one's eye (wash out immediately with plain water) will be unpleasant, but is unlikely to do any harm.

WASHING THE APPLES

Once the apples are ready for pressing they need to be washed. Many ciderists simply wash them in clean water. As an added precaution against unwanted organisms, however, they can be rinsed in a weak, 0.5 per cent sodium metabisulphite solution and then rinsed again in clean water. That is my practice.

Those ciderists who ferment relying upon naturally occurring yeasts rather than adding cultured yeasts, may worry that rinsing their apples, particularly if the rinsing is preceded by weak sterilisation, will destroy the naturally occurring yeasts. Of course it will kill any yeasts that are on the skin of the apple but the yeasts also reside inside the apple itself. In any event, it is probable that the yeasts that are operative in a natural fermentation will come from the general environment and not specifically from the apple.

Above left: Examining the apples before washing.

Above: The apples are first put into a weak sterilising solution and then rinsed in plain water.

Some apples are put aside and cut for examination.

REMOVING DISEASED, ROTTEN OR DAMAGED APPLES

Washing the apples is also an opportunity to examine them and to remove any diseased or rotten apples that have been overlooked when they were gathered, and apples that appear to have been damaged by insects or pests. Apples float in water but very rotten apples may sink to the bottom. A hole in an apple might indicate worm or insect damage within. All one has to do is to cut open the apple and decide whether it is worth pressing or not. Generally, if one wouldn't be willing to eat the apple one shouldn't press it. Just as when eating an apple, however, it is often possible to cut away the damaged part of the fruit and press the good part remaining. Whether this is worthwhile depends on how determined one is to obtain the maximum possible yield from one's apples. Otherwise, damaged apples should simply be discarded.

SCRATTING AND MILLING

It would take a colossal force, beyond what may be generated by conventional cider presses, to press whole apples. So, the apples must first be reduced to smaller pieces. This is referred to as 'scratting' or 'milling'.

A manual scratter in operation.

MANUAL SCRATTING

For very small quantities of apples this can be done simply by cutting the apples into quarters, placing them into a bucket and smashing them with a heavy lump of timber. For any significant volume of apples, however, this method will take a disproportionate amount of time and effort. The next level of sophistication is to use a manual scratter, which will normally consist of two rollers with contra-rotating blunt spikes. The rollers are turned by a circular handle and the apples are manually fed or poured between the contra-rotating rollers. If a manual scratter is being used, it is still necessary first to quarter the apples to ensure that they will run through the scratter easily and be crushed sufficiently to allow them to be pressed.

MECHANICAL MILLS

Pouring apples into an electric mill.

Commercial cider producers have for many years used motorised mills with revolving blades to chop, or mill, the apples into smaller pieces, operating like giant food processors or garden shredders. Recently affordable electric mills have become available which are suitable for the domestic ciderist. They obviate the need for prior cutting into quarters and are, in my view, a very worthwhile investment for all levels of domestic cidermaking except perhaps the very small. I should certainly recommend an electric mill for anybody who hopes to make 100 litres of cider or more.

Those with a talent for DIY might make their own mills by adapting garden shredders. Advice and shared experience are available on the internet (see Appendix 6). One should, however, sound a note of caution. Apple juice and cider are both quite strongly acidic and so many materials dissolve if soaked in them. In general, only glass, stainless steel or food-grade plastic should be allowed to be in direct contact with the juice. Wood may be used but it is often difficult to keep clean and free from spoilage bacteria. Wood is often used both in basket presses and in rack and cloth presses, for example, where it will usually be coated with polyurethane varnish to aid cleaning.

Above left:
The pomace
coming from the
electric mill.

Above: A Fruit
Shark mill.

PRESSING
Once the apples have been scratted or milled the resulting pulp is called pomace and is ready to be pressed. The apples having been separated according to their cultivar, the pomace from each cultivar should be pressed separately and the resulting juice kept separate from the juice of apples of other cultivars. Presses suitable for use by the domestic ciderist are of three main types.

Pomace ready
to be taken to
the press.

BASKET PRESSES
In the basket press a slatted wooden basket sits on a receiving tray. A rotating screw screws down a wooden plate, which presses the apples. The wooden plate has a metal area to receive the screw. The screw is turned by means of a long metal handle. The apple juice runs into a tray and out of a hole or into a pipe into the receiving vessel. The receiving vessel is either

Right: Juice being collected from a basket press.

Below: A basket press with a manual scratter.

the vessel in which the juice is to be fermented or, more usually, some smaller vessel such as a bowl or bucket.

RACK AND CLOTH PRESSES

If one intends to make, say, 200 litres or more of cider, pressing with a basket press will be very

A rack and cloth press at Manor Farm, Limington, 1934.

time-consuming. One is unlikely to achieve 50 per cent efficiency with such a press and a large amount of juice, which will remain in the spent pomace, will be wasted. Rack and cloth presses have been used for several hundred years. They contain a 'bed' or square plate on which is laid a slatted square rack. A frame (known as a 'form') is then laid on the rack and a press cloth is laid diagonally on the form so that the corners protrude from each side of the square. Pomace is scooped onto the cloth and distributed evenly.

A publican pressing with a rack and cloth press, Somersetshire, early twentieth century.

Above: A rack and cloth press at Westowe Manor Farm, ready for pressing: the juice is already flowing.

Above right: Lowering the press.

Right: Pressing in progress.

Far right: The cheese pressed thin.

The corners of the cloth are then folded over to form an envelope. The form is removed, a new rack is added and the process is repeated. Each layer was traditionally known as a 'hair'. When a pile of ten to twelve hairs has been made they form collectively a 'cheese' and are ready for pressing. There will be a plate above the cheese. Usually this will be movable although sometimes it is the bed which is the movable part. The movable plate is pressed down on the cheese, either manually with a screw thread or bottle jack or with electric power by a hydraulic ram. Rack and cloth presses are available from commercial manufacturers. Those powered by a hydraulic ram tend to be of a size catering for a level of production that is too large for domestic ciderists. Again, those with a talent for DIY might build their own and there are a number of designs available on the internet for those who wish to do so.

Above left: A modern rack and cloth press.

Top right: A hair of a cheese being prepared.

Above: Juice being pressed from a cheese.

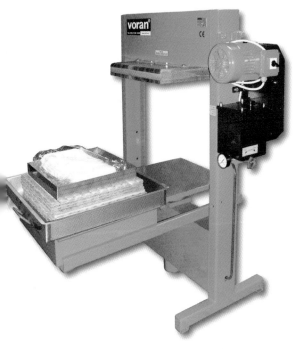

Left: A modern hydraulic rack and cloth press.

HYDROPRESSES

An alternative that has recently become available from commercial manufacturers is the hydropress consisting of a stainless-steel drum and a central heavy rubber inner bag. A straining sack is placed around the inner sides of the steel drum. The sack is then filled with pomace and a metal lid screwed down to the drum. The rubber inner bag is filled by connecting an ordinary garden hose to the press. The bag expands and presses the pomace against the outer drum. When I first saw these presses I couldn't believe that filling the rubber bag with the water from an ordinary garden hose could create sufficient pressure for the pressing. The manufacturers claim only 60 per cent efficiency for these presses but my own experience is that they will extract juice at 70 per cent efficiency. For the domestic ciderist who wishes to press 200 litres of juice or more they are an ideal press, being simple to operate and easy to clean.

Top left:
Filling the
hydropress.

Top right and
above: The
hydropress uses
water pressure
from an ordinary
mains supply and
creates a nice flow
of juice.

RECEIVING VESSELS

Whichever type of press is used, when the press is loaded, the weight of the pomace will immediately cause some juice to flow from it and so the receiving vessel should be in place before the press is loaded with pomace. A second receiving vessel should be at hand so that the vessels may be swapped over when they are full or when one wants to begin transferring the juice to the fermentation bin. The receiving vessels need be no more sophisticated than food-grade plastic bowls but they need to be of a size appropriate to the output of the particular press used.

When pouring the newly pressed juice into the fermentation bin it is a good idea to strain it. It is very difficult to exclude all of the pomace from the juice and occasionally wasps and other insects will find their way into it.

Left: Changing receiving vessels.

Above: Pouring the juice into a fermentation bin. Note the stainless-steel sieve.

STORAGE DURING FERMENTATION AND MATURATION

Once it has been obtained by pressing, the apple juice is transferred from the receiving vessel to the vessel in which it is to be fermented – a fermentation bin. At this stage the pressed juice is referred to as 'must'. Fermentation bins should be as large as can be conveniently handled, subject to the need to fill each vessel to the brim and, if more than one blend is to be made, to deal with each blend separately. After fermentation, the cider will be matured in similarly large vessels for some time before it is either bottled or put into a dispensing container. We have already seen that, because cider is an acid liquid that will dissolve many solids, there is a limited range of materials (stainless steel, glass, food-grade plastic, and wood) which are suitable to be in contact with the fermenting must or resulting cider for any length of time. In the past, wood casks were used but these have been superseded by other materials because wood is difficult to clean thoroughly, is permeable to air and will itself impart flavours to the cider. Unless only very small quantities of cider are to be made (50 litres or less), glass will not be suitable because it will be too heavy, too expensive and, probably, too fragile. Stainless steel is the best material and stainless-steel tanks are used by many craft commercial ciderists and by large producers of industrial ciders. Unfortunately, stainless-steel tanks are very expensive and it is difficult to obtain tanks with a capacity of less than 60 litres. That amount of apple juice will weigh more than 60 kg and the weight of the vessel will be added to that. Unless it is possible to arrange one's cidermaking area so that the must or cider can be pumped from vessel to vessel, it will be necessary to move full fermentation bins from time to time. Storage vessels of 60 kg are too heavy to be easily moved by one person. What is more, a unit size of 60 litres is probably going to be too large for most domestic ciderists, both because the last vessel to be filled might have a large amount of unused space and because, if one wishes to experiment with different blends, one will have to do so in very large units. Of course, the latter difficulty could be overcome by having a mixture of stainless-steel bins and smaller storage vessels made from other materials.

Food-grade plastic fermentation bins, which can be fitted with an airlock during fermentation and can be tightly sealed once the must has been fermented to dryness, are therefore the normal method of storage during fermentation and maturation for the domestic ciderist. Those with sufficient space to arrange their vessels so that the must or cider can be pumped from vessel to vessel can, subject to expense, use stainless steel.

Such fermentation bins usually have a stated capacity of either 25 or 30 litres (or similar capacities in gallons). Actually, their capacity, when filled to the brim, will usually be significantly more than the stated amount. So a fermentation bin sold as having a capacity of 30 litres might have a capacity when completely full of almost 35 litres.

All plastic has some degree of permeability by air but food-grade plastic fermentation bins are sold by most home-brew shops in a thickness (about 1.6 mm) which will allow the cider to be kept for up to a year without any appreciable deterioration through oxidation, so long as the vessel is kept completely full so as to exclude air. Fermentation bins made of extra-thick food-grade plastic (about 2.5 mm) are more expensive but the amount of air permeability is so low that cider may be kept for several years without deterioration.

During fermentation the cider will lose volume to evaporation and the release of carbon dioxide. It is sensible to ferment some of the must in vessels of a smaller volume, for example glass demijohns, so that one can use that cider for topping up the larger vessels.

4: MEASUREMENT, BLENDING AND ADDITIONS

I N THIS and the following chapter we consider making dry cider – that is, cider where virtually all of the sugars in the must are converted into alcohol through fermentation. Chapter 6 deals with variations that are made in order to make medium-dry, semi-sweet, sweet and sparkling ('conditioned') ciders.

MEASURING

Having pressed the juice from each type of cultivar, one must then assess it. That means measuring sugar content and acidity and assessing, by taste, tannin and flavour.

SUGAR CONTENT: DENSITY

When in fermentation yeasts convert the sugars in the must into ethyl alcohol and carbon dioxide, approximately equal amounts by weight of alcohol and carbon dioxide are created. Because carbon dioxide is a gas, most of it is released from the must in bubbles, so fermentation results in the sugar in the must being replaced by alcohol. Sugar is denser than alcohol; therefore fermentation results in a decrease in the average density of the must. By measuring the initial and final density, one can calculate the amount of alcohol produced. There are various methods of expressing density.

SPECIFIC GRAVITY AND ALCOHOL CONTENT

Specific gravity expresses density by reference to water measured at a standard temperature of 15°C and pressure of 1 bar on a scale on which distilled water is 1,000. Specific gravities above 1,000 are denser than water and those below 1,000 are less dense. Apple juice typically consists of slightly more than 80 per cent water and 8–15 per cent sugar with the balance consisting of various dissolved solids, acid and other ingredients.

The primary phase of fermentation in which the must ferments vigorously, creating a froth.

When the must is fully fermented the only change that will have significantly affected its density is the replacement of sugar by alcohol. If all of the sugar is fermented it will have a specific gravity a little below that of water, being somewhere between 995 and 998. So by measuring the initial specific gravity of a must one can estimate both the amount of sugar in the must and the proportion of alcohol it will contain if it is fully fermented to dryness.

Specific gravity at 15°C	Potential alcohol by volume (per cent)	Sugar by weight in 1 litre of must (grams)
998	0.0	0
1,000	0.2	3
1,005	0.7	12
1,010	1.2	21
1,015	1.8	30
1,020	2.3	39
1,025	2.9	49
1,030	3.5	59
1,035	4.1	70
1,040	4.7	81
1,045	5.4	92
1,050	6.1	103
1,055	6.8	115
1,060	7.5	128
1,065	8.2	140
1,070	9.0	153
1,075	9.8	166
1,080	10.6	180
1,085	11.4	194
1,090	12.2	208
1,095	13.1	223
1,100	14.0	238

These figures are only approximate because they involve making assumptions both about the behaviour of the yeast in the must and the materials other than water and sugars present in it. For excise duty purposes a more accurate method of calculation is necessary, which requires the services of a professional laboratory. The domestic ciderist is not concerned with excise duty but the alcohol content of his cider is important for three reasons: firstly, because it affects the perceived flavour; secondly, because it confers the cider's intoxicating power; and thirdly, because the higher the percentage of alcohol the more that spoilage organisms are inhibited. For all these purposes, an accuracy of +/- 0.5 per cent is sufficient and it is possible to achieve that level of accuracy without laboratory testing.

THE HYDROMETER

Alcohol content may be estimated to this degree of accuracy from the measurement of specific gravity by means of a hydrometer. A hydrometer

A hydrometer for measuring specific gravity is placed in the liquid to be measured and then read.

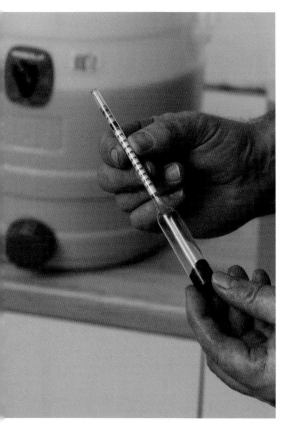

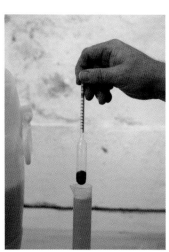

is a slender, sealed, blown-glass (or, sometimes, plastic) tube weighted at one end with lead shot and with one or more scales on the upper stem. It is floated in the liquid to be tested and the higher it floats the greater the density of the liquid. It is important that when the hydrometer is placed into the liquid, it is spun to dislodge any gas bubbles which would otherwise increase its buoyancy and therefore give an artificially high reading. A liquid has a tendency to form a convex curve when in contact with unfilled glass. That curve is referred to as the 'meniscus'. When reading the hydrometer, therefore, one should determine the point at which the surface of the liquid cuts the stem rather than reading the scale at the top of the meniscus.

Most hydrometers assume pressure of a single atmosphere and a temperature of 15°C. Variations in pressure are unlikely to affect the reading significantly. Variations in temperature can have some significance. Variation from the target temperature of +/-5°C may alter the specific gravity reading by one unit. One adds to the specific gravity reading for temperatures above the target temperature and subtracts for temperatures below it. So if a specific gravity reading is taken with a hydrometer in a must with a temperature of 20°C, 1 degree of specific gravity would be added to the result.

The larger its range the more difficult it is to read the hydrometer's scale accurately. The most suitable hydrometers available are those primarily aimed at winemaking, but even they have a smaller scale and therefore a larger range than is really suitable for cidermaking because they must deal with specific gravities of 1,120 or more. An ideal range is from 990 to 1,100 but it is not always easy to find hydrometers that are calibrated in this way.

SPECIFIC GRAVITIES OF APPLE JUICE

Cider apples produce average specific gravities of 1,055–1,060 and specific gravities above 1,075 are rare. Specific gravities for apple juice, however, have been recorded of almost 1,100, which would give alcohol by volume (ABV) of 14.0 per cent (see page 48). Culinary apples are on average in the range 1,035–1,040 and table apples in the range 1,040–1,050. There will be large variations between cultivars and, in respect of the same cultivar, between trees and, in respect of the same tree, between harvests. As we have seen, the time at which the apple is harvested and the time between harvesting and pressing also significantly affect sugar levels.

TARGET ALCOHOL CONTENT

There is no single correct alcohol level for cider. Under excise duty law, cider made for sale with an ABV of 8.5 per cent or more is subject to the duties that apply to made wine. The domestic ciderist need not concern himself with this, however, as his concern is entirely with quality.

Most ciderists would agree that an alcohol level of less than 6 per cent is too low for craft cider and will also provide insufficient protection against spoilage organisms during storage. Most ciderists would probably also agree that 10 per cent alcohol is too high. Within these broad limits alcohol content needs to be related to the style, sweetness, acidity and body of the cider and the personal taste of the drinker.

ADJUSTING FOR POTENTIAL ALCOHOL

Potential alcohol content can be adjusted by blending juice from different cultivars. Achieving the correct proportion, however, may mean excluding some of the juice from the must. There may also have to be a compromise between achieving the correct level of sugar and the correct level of acidity, tannin and flavours. An alternative is to add sugar if the must lacks the desired amount of sugar, or to dilute it with water if it has too much. Many ciderists prefer to allow the composition of their juice to determine the final alcoholic strength; but if there is insufficient sugar to give at least 6 per cent alcohol – requiring a starting specific gravity of 1,049 – one risks spoilage if one does not adjust the sugar level.

Diluting the cider is normally undertaken once fermentation has been completed, unless the sugar level is extremely high (a starting gravity above 1,075), when high concentrations of alcohol towards the end of fermentation might inhibit the activity of the yeast. Supplementing the sugars, however, must be done before the completion of fermentation. In calculating the correct amount to add, account should be taken of the volume of the added sugar solution. Ordinary white, granulated cane sugar can be used for this purpose. There is no need to use the glucose stocked by many home-brew shops because yeast breaks down sucrose into glucose and fructose during the process of fermentation. There is, however, no reason why glucose should not be used and it is often cheaper than household sugar.

Many ciderists object strongly to the addition of sugar and, in particular, glucose to cider. As we have seen, industrial cider is often referred to disparagingly by ciderists as 'glucose wine' because so much of its alcoholic content comes from the glucose that is added to it rather than from the naturally occurring fructose in the apple juice. The inferior flavour of industrial cider, however, does not arise from the use of glucose but from the dilution of apple juice, the use of concentrates and additives and the methods of its fermentation and storage. Fermented sucrose and glucose do not have any distinctive flavour characteristics and so adding glucose dissolved in water to a must will have no effect on the flavour of the resulting cider other than the normal effect on perceived flavour of higher concentrations of alcohol and whatever effect on flavour the dilution may have. A dilution of less than 15 per cent does not affect to any significant degree the perceived flavour of cider.

ADJUSTING SUGAR CONTENT: AN EXAMPLE

It may be helpful to give an example of adjusting a blend in respect of sugar content. Mr Shekar hopes to make a cider which will be 6.5 per cent alcohol and 0.4 per cent total acid. He makes juice from apples of two cultivars as follows:

Cultivar	Amount of juice (litres)	Specific gravity	Total acid (per cent)
A	100	1,060	0.2
B	200	1,040	0.5

Mr Shekar is considering three differing approaches:

1. To blend all of his apple juice and accept whatever results;
2. To blend all of his A apples with sufficient B apples to bring total alcohol to 6.5 per cent;
3. As in (1) but to add sufficient glucose solution to bring the alcohol to 6.5 per cent.

OPTION 1

The combined must will have a specific gravity of 1,046.67 (1,060 x 100/300) + (1,040 x 200/300)) giving potential alcohol of just 5.6 per cent. It will have total acid of 0.4 per cent ((0.2 per cent x 100/300) + (0.5 per cent x 200/300)).

OPTION 2

To achieve potential alcohol of 6.5 per cent he needs a specific gravity of 1,053, so the mixture must contain 100 litres of the A juice and 53.84 litres of the B juice with 146.16 litres not being made into cider. It will have a total acid of just 0.3 per cent ((0.2 per cent x 100 /153.84) + (0.5 per cent x 53.84/153.84).

OPTION 3

Mr Shekar would add a solution of glucose and water of 5 litres which will bring the total volume of juice to 305 litres. The table on page 48 suggests that 1 litre of juice with a potential alcohol of 6.5 per cent will have 109.9 grams of sugar in it. So 305 litres would require 33.5 kg of sugar. The 200 litres of juice from the B apples which have a specific gravity of 1,040 will have 16.2 kg of sugar dissolved in them. The 100 litres of the A juice with a specific gravity of 1,060 will have 12.8 kg of sugar in them. So Mr Shekar's must will already contain 29.0 kg of dissolved sugar. He would therefore dissolve 4.5 kg (33.5 – 16.2 – 12.8) kg of sugar in 2.5 litres of water and then add sufficient further water to make the mixture up to 5 litres. He would then boil the sugar solution to sterilise it and, after it had cooled, add it to the must. The minor dilution caused by the addition of the sugar solution would reduce the total acid percentage marginally below 0.4 per cent.

ADDITIONS OVER TIME

Because the required sugar content for a given potential ABV and the amount of sugar in a liquid at the start of fermentation can be calculated where the specific gravity and the volume of the liquid are known, one may calculate the potential ABV of any mixture of liquids where the specific gravity and volumes of the original liquid and of any additions to it are known. That means it is possible to add apple juice or sugar solution over the course of the fermentation and still be able to estimate final alcohol content.

CYSER

Drinks made from fermenting together apple juice and honey are known as cyser. The honey contains floral esters, trace elements and pollens which impart smoothness and richness to the flavour and bouquet of the resulting cyser. Honey is essentially a syrup of glucose and fructose and therefore, where sugar would otherwise be added to the must to increase its potential alcohol, honey could be substituted. Honey contains approximately 80 per cent sugar and so 1.25 kg of honey is equivalent to 1 kg of pure sugar. So in Option 3 of our example (see page 52), Mr Shekar might have added 5.625 kg (4.5 kg x 100/80) of honey to his must instead of 4.5 kg of sugar.

Unless the honey has been pasteurised it will contain micro-organisms which may be harmful. The pH of honey varies between 3.2 and 4.5. A solution of unpasteurised honey with a pH of 3.8 or less may be sulphited with the amount of sodium metabisulphite appropriate to its pH (see page 59) and then covered and allowed to stand for a few hours before it is added to the must. A solution of unpasteurised honey with a pH above 3.8 should be pasteurised at this stage. Almost all varieties of honey can be used except eucalyptus honey which imparts an unpleasant flavour to the cyser which is not apparent in the flavour of the honey. Light, delicately flavoured honeys are to be preferred; for example, honey made from clover. Honey made from heather tends to be strongly flavoured and should be used with caution.

MEASURING ACTUAL ALCOHOL CONTENT

As we have seen, measuring alcohol content to a sufficient degree of accuracy for excise duty purposes requires the services of a professional laboratory. The alcohol content of a liquid can be measured outside the professional laboratory, however, to an accuracy of +/- 0.5 per cent, both by a refractometer (which measures the refractive index of the liquid, the alcohol content of which is to be determined) in conjunction with an accurate specific gravity reading, and by an ebulliometer (using a method based on determining the boiling point of the liquid). Both are expensive. As alcohol

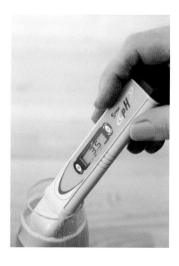

content can be estimated from initial and final specific gravities with scarcely less accuracy, few domestic ciderists find the expense worthwhile.

ACIDITY

Solutions with a pH below 7 are acidic and those with a pH above 7 are alkaline, so an increase in pH reduces acidity. Test papers can be used to measure pH; these are dipped in the solution to be measured and turn different colours according to the degree of acidity or alkalinity of the solution. These provide a reasonable, low-cost method of measurement, but it is sometimes difficult to match the colour to the colour strip provided by the manufacturers. Test papers are best read in daylight; if that cannot be done, then the next-best option is to read them under the light of

Measuring pH with
a pH meter.

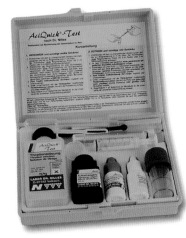

Sulphur dioxide
and acid
testing kit.

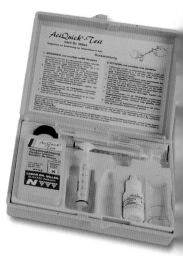

a halogen lamp. An alternative is to buy a pH meter. The meters need to be calibrated frequently but most have a digital display and are easy to read.

The pH of a juice should be in the range 3.2–3.8. A pH below 3.2 is likely to result in a juice that is unpleasantly acidic. A reading above 3.8 is unlikely to give sufficient protection against spoilage.

Total acid is measured by titration. Titration testing kits are available from most home-brew shops. An ideal value for total acidity is 0.4 per cent. Total acidity is normally expressed as parts per thousand ('ppt') of equivalent tartaric or sulphuric acid. The acid in cider is primarily malic acid. A solution that is 4.0 ppt of malic acid will be equivalent in acidity to a solution which is 4.5 ppt of tartaric acid or 2.9 ppt of sulphuric acid.

As noted previously (see Chapter 3), pH is the best measure of the juice's protection from spoilage and should be in the range 3.2–3.8, while total acidity has the better correlation with taste. As there is a rough correlation between pH and total acidity, achieving a pH in the middle of the acceptable range (that is, 3.4–3.6) should ensure that the total acidity is also in the correct range.

What should be done if the pH of the juice is outside this range? The first approach is through blending. If, however, the available juice does not have the desired level of acidity, under-acidity can be adjusted by the careful addition of malic acid, which is available from most home-brew shops. The acid should be added in steps of 1 gram per litre and the pH measured after each addition. As it is difficult to weigh 1 gram, one might make up a solution of 10 grams of acid in 100 ml of boiled water and add liquid in 10 ml amounts using a pipette.

Over-acidity can be reduced by dilution, by malolactic fermentation and by the addition of potassium carbonate.

There are, of course, limits to the degree to which one would wish to dilute cider. The aim is to have a minimum apple juice content of 85 per cent. The pH scale is a logarithmic scale and so changes in pH are not proportionate to changes in volume. A 10 per cent dilution, therefore, will not give a 10 per cent increase in pH. Again, one should dilute in stages until the target pH is achieved.

Malolactic fermentation will be covered in the next chapter because it takes place when alcoholic fermentation has ended. Malolactic fermentation results in the conversion of malic acid

Acids, including malic acid.

into lactic acid. Lactic acid is half as acidic as malic acid and, therefore, one of the effects of malolactic fermentation is a reduction in total acid which can be as much as 45 per cent (because the acid in apple juice typically consists of 90 per cent malic acid and 10 per cent quinic acid). It will also increase pH. As the success, or otherwise, of the malolactic fermentation will determine whether, and, if so, to what extent, dilution is required, where one intends to allow or to stimulate malolactic fermentation, dilution should be delayed until that fermentation is complete.

Acid can be chemically neutralised by the addition of potassium carbonate. Again, additions should be made in increments of 0.1 per cent. One might, therefore, reduce the acidity of a juice that is likely to remain over-acidic after dilution and malolactic fermentation, by the addition of potassium carbonate. Potassium carbonate affects the flavour of cider adversely because it remains in solution. The maximum dose that can be added without having a major effect on flavour is 0.3 per cent by weight of the liquid to which it is added. This may not sufficiently reduce the acidity of very acid musts. My view is that the use of potassium carbonate should be avoided. Cider should not be made from culinary apples alone, and if it is made from a reasonable mix of culinary and table apples (or from cider apples if they are available), it is unlikely to be so acidic after dilution and malolactic fermentation that it will not be pleasantly drinkable and refreshing.

OTHER ADDITIONS TO THE MUST: YEAST

The question of fermenting with naturally occurring yeasts or cultured yeasts divides ciderists. Those who favour the use of naturally occurring yeasts say that they produce a more complex and more interesting flavour because there is a succession of different types of yeast involved in the fermentation process. In the fermentation of cultured yeasts, however, conditions are deliberately created in which a single variety of cultured yeast is allowed to become quickly dominant and it is said that the result is rather monochrome. On the other hand, cultured yeasts have been developed specifically for fermentation, although of wine and not cider, and are, as a result, reliable. The development of cultured yeasts requires a very considerable investment and there is not yet a sufficient market for yeast developed specifically for cider fermentation to stimulate that investment.

FERMENTATION WITH NATURALLY OCCURRING YEASTS

Apple juice contains a high number of apiculate (or lemon-shaped) yeasts. (The most common form of apiculate yeasts in cider are *Kloeckera apiculata* and apiculate yeasts are often referred to by ciderists simply as 'Kloeckera'.) Normally, fermentation by these yeasts will start within hours of the juice

being pressed. Generally, apiculate yeasts cannot survive in concentrations of alcohol of more than 2–4 per cent and so they will die in the early stages of fermentation. The must and the general environment will also include small numbers of yeasts of the species *Saccharomyces cerevisiae* which will multiply slowly until, as the alcohol level moves above 2 per cent, they come to dominate the fermentation.

Cultured yeast.

FERMENTATION WITH CULTURED YEASTS

Cultured yeasts sold as suitable for cidermaking have in fact been developed for white wine. Different strains of yeast will produce notably different flavours. Cider is fermented at lower temperatures and for longer periods than wine and so yeasts which have been developed to be optimal for wine production may not be optimal for cider production. So it is a good idea to search for yeasts designed for wines of colder regions such as Champagne or the regions of Germany. Champagne yeasts, which are of the species *Saccharomyces bayanus*, ferment to extreme dryness. They are therefore unsuitable for those who prefer a hint of sweetness to their cider but are very useful for those making bone-dry or sparkling cider. Brewer's or baker's yeast should not be used in cidermaking.

METABISULPHITE

Both the must and the surrounding environment may contain spoilage yeasts, moulds and bacteria which, if they were to develop, would adversely affect the flavour of the cider. These may be inhibited or killed by the addition of sodium or potassium metabisulphite. Many craft ciderists object to the addition of metabisulphite to the must because it detracts from the purity of their product. As we have seen, however, sulphur dioxide has been used in cidermaking since at least the seventeenth century and may have been used since ancient times.

During fermentation, sulphur dioxide binds itself to various chemicals that are produced by the yeast in the fermentation process. So if sulphur dioxide is added only near the beginning of fermentation, by the end of fermentation all of the sulphur dioxide should be 'bound'. A small minority of people have an intolerance to unbound sulphur dioxide. EU regulations restrict the amount of sulphur dioxide which can be added to cider and wine to 200 parts per million (ppm). Such restrictions need not concern the domestic ciderist although he may wish to measure the free sulphur dioxide of his finished product to avoid inadvertently provoking allergic reactions in those who drink his cider. Because sulphur dioxide intolerance is rare and is not life-threatening, there is generally no necessity for him to do so. Testing kits for doing so are available from wine- and cidermaking equipment suppliers.

The amount of metabisulphite that is required to protect the must will vary according to the must's acidity. The table on page 59 gives a suggested dosage for musts with pH readings up to and including 3.8.

We have seen that the amount of sulphur dioxide in a solution is expressed in ppm and that sodium metabisulphite is composed of 50 per cent or more sulphur dioxide. The stock solution of 10 per cent sodium metabisulphite recommended in Chapter 3 would contain a little more than 5 per cent sulphur dioxide, so the table on page 59 also gives the number of millilitres per litre of stock solution equivalent to the required dose of sulphur dioxide.

Campden tablets.

CAMPDEN TABLETS

Campden tablets are tablets containing a measured dose of sodium metabisulphite of 0.44 grams – sufficient, when dissolved in 1 gallon of water, to result in a solution of sulphur dioxide of 50 ppm. Their name derives from the town of Chipping Campden in Gloucestershire where the Fruit and Vegetable Preserving Research Station, at which they were first developed in the 1920s, was situated. Where weak solutions of sodium metabisulphite are required, as when one sulphites a must at the beginning of fermentation, Campden tablets are a convenient way of adding a precise amount of sulphite to a solution. Using them for making up a stock solution for sterilising equipment, however, would be an expensive way of purchasing the required sodium metabisulphite.

Recommended dosages of Sodium Dioxide			
Juice (pH)	Sulphur dioxide needed (ppm)	10 per cent sodium metabisulphite stock solution (ml per litre)	Campden tablets per 5 litres
Below 3.0	None	None	None
3.1	50	1.0	1
3.2	60	1.2	1
3.3	72	1.4	2
3.4	85	1.7	2
3.5	103	2.1	2
3.6	125	2.5	3
3.7	151	3.0	3
3.8	184	3.7	4

ADDING METABISULPHITE WHEN FERMENTING WITH CULTURED YEASTS

Adding metabisulphite to the must, therefore, is a way of preventing the development of unwanted yeasts and bacteria which may otherwise adversely affect the flavour. It will also, depending on the level, inhibit or destroy the apiculate yeasts. This is not a concern where cultured yeast is used because the aim is then to ensure that the cultured yeast quickly becomes dominant. Indeed it is an advantage, because it ensures that consistency and predictability which are the purpose of using cultured yeasts. As the sulphur dioxide becomes bound its effect is reduced. So it is common practice to add metabisulphite immediately to the must on its being pressed and to add the cultured yeast 24 hours later when the inhibiting effects of the metabisulphite will have reduced.

YEAST STARTERS

Cultured yeasts can be grown independently of the must in a 'yeast starter' allowing them to have multiplied considerably already when the starter is added to the must.

A yeast starter is made in a sterilised demijohn. First, 300 grams of sugar are added to 2 litres of water. One then boils the solution, covers it, allows it to cool and adds one level teaspoon of yeast nutrient. The nutrients required by yeasts are thiamine and amino acids. Home-brew shops sell mixtures of ammonium sulphate and thiamine in a powdered form, normally under the description 'yeast nutrient'. The mixture is then made up to 3 litres by the addition of further boiled and cooled water. Alternatively, one could heat 3 litres of apple juice to 66°C, cover it and allow it to cool and add yeast nutrient. One would then add yeast according to the manufacturer's instructions for the volume of cider to which it is to be added. The demijohn would then be plugged with cotton wool and left to stand in a warmish place (15–18°C). It will not matter if more yeast is used than the manufacturer recommends for the volume of must being fermented, but one must take account of the volume of the yeast starter in proportion to the volume of the must, as a large volume of starter might dilute the must significantly.

ADDING METABISULPHITE TO MUSTS FERMENTED BY NATURAL YEASTS

It is also a wise precaution against spoilage to add metabisulphite to the must where the must is to be fermented by natural yeasts. Sulphite at the levels given in the table, however, would seriously inhibit the development of apiculate yeasts and retard the development of the *saccharomyces cerevisiae*. The result might be to reduce the complexity of flavour, which is the aim of natural fermentation, and also to increase oxidation because it will take longer for a carbon dioxide blanket to form. For that reason only half of the quantities given in the table should be added.

A yeast starter. Notice the cotton wool bung.

OTHER ADDITIONS TO THE MUST: NUTRIENTS

We have already seen that yeasts require thiamine and amino acids as nutrients. Apple juice is very much lower in these nutrients than grape juice, which is one of the reasons why cider fermentation takes longer than the fermentation of wine. The quantities of nutrients in apple juice vary significantly. There are variations between cultivars and differences in soil, and orcharding practice (in particular the use of fertilisers) can lead to significant variations in nutrient content even between juices derived from the same cultivar. Many ciderists routinely add nutrients at the start of fermentation to help the fermentation get going. Others do not do so and find that fermentation still proceeds without trouble.

The addition of nutrients is a traditional part of cidermaking. It was once a common practice to put pieces of meat into the fermenting vessel; these would be broken down into amino nitrogen and vitamins by the action of the acid in the juice. It is a picturesque but untrue tale that rats were put in the cider for the same purpose.

If one wishes to avoid adding nutrients but also wishes to ensure that the fermentation proceeds successfully, a compromise is not to add nutrients to the must before fermentation but to allow the fermentation to proceed and to add further nutrients only in the event that the fermentation 'sticks'. A fermentation 'sticks' when it stops before all of the sugar in the must has been converted into alcohol; that is, before it is fermented to complete dryness.

OTHER ADDITIONS TO THE MUST: PECTOLYTIC ENZYMES

Apple juice contains high levels of pectins (1.0–1.5 per cent), which can result in a gel being formed, causing hazes. Pectins are soluble in water but are precipitated by alcohol so pectin hazes tend to form towards the end of fermentation. Table apples and apples that have been stored for a long time tend to have particularly high levels of pectin. Both apples and yeasts contain natural enzymes which may break down the pectins during fermentation but they may not be sufficient in themselves. Home-brew shops sell pectolytic enzymes to break down pectins and prevent the formation of pectin gels. The most common brand name under which pectolytic enzymes are sold is 'Pectolase'. The pectolytic enzyme will not work once the haze is formed so it should be added, in accordance with the manufacturer's instructions, immediately after the juice is pressed.

5: FROM FERMENTATION TO TASTING

FERMENTATION

1. The lag phase

The lag phase takes place in the period between the juice being pressed, or, where cultured yeasts are used, the cultured yeasts being added to the must and the first visible signs of fermentation. The must is said to be inoculated with the yeast and the yeast is therefore referred to as the 'inoculum'. During this period, while the yeasts are establishing themselves, they require a very large amount of oxygen and, therefore, a source of oxygen in addition to that which is dissolved in the must. This is a phase of aerobic fermentation so the fermentation vessel cannot be entirely stopped. To prevent contamination from outside organisms, however, the vessel can be loosely stopped with a cotton-wool plug.

2. The primary fermentation

Next is the phase of primary fermentation, when carbon dioxide rises to the surface of the must in bubbles which rapidly become very vigorous. The vigour of the fermentation creates a froth and in some cases the froth may rise considerably in the vessel. In filling the fermentation vessel with must, therefore, it should not at first be filled to the brim but at least 10 to 13 centimetres should be left to give room for the froth. Carbon dioxide is heavier than air and therefore when it is released it sits on the must as a blanket, protecting it from contamination by micro-organisms but also preventing access to the oxygen in the air. The primary fermentation, therefore, depends upon the oxygen obtained in the process of fermentation itself by the breakdown of sugars. It is an anaerobic fermentation.

3. The secondary fermentation

After a while the vigour of the fermentation reduces as the yeasts' activity is inhibited by the increasing amounts of alcohol in the must; the amount of carbon dioxide released also reduces. This is the secondary fermentation phase. At this stage the carbon dioxide blanket will thin and it is necessary to protect the fermenting must from contact with the air by topping up the vessel with further must and closing it with a fermentation lock. Sulphite solution is added to the fermentation lock to destroy any micro-organisms which might otherwise pass through the lock. Occasionally, a must that has apparently reached the secondary phrase begins to ferment vigorously again and bubbles up through the fermentation lock. When it subsides it will bring into the must the liquid in the fermentation lock. For this reason, only a weak (1 per cent) sulphite solution is used for filling fermentation locks.

Above: Cider fermenting in a thick-walled fermentation bin with fermentation lock.

Fermenter with fermentation lock.

Fermentation locks should be added as soon as the initial frothing has subsided. This may be only two to five days after pressing, or in the case of those using cultured yeasts, after inoculation with the yeast.

TEMPERATURE

Traditionally, cider has been fermented in unheated cider houses or in the open. Because cider is normally made in late autumn the initial temperature of the must would have been quite low and would have reduced as fermentation continued over the winter.

The fermentative ability of cultured wine yeasts declines in temperatures above about 30°C and naturally occurring yeasts will normally have a heat tolerance significantly below this. Up to the limit of their heat tolerance, the higher the temperature the quicker the fermentation. It is generally accepted that cider benefits from a longer and slower fermentation than wine. Many ciderists simply ferment their cider in unheated buildings or in the open, in the traditional way, and allow the average temperature to be determined by the vagaries of the climate. Some yeasts will continue to ferment at temperatures as low as 5°C. If the temperature falls too low, the yeast will become dormant and the fermentation will stick. Even if the temperature drops to a level where the fermentation sticks, however, it will normally restart when temperatures rise again in the spring.

If the temperature of the must is controlled artificially then a cool temperature of 15°C or below is best. Many yeasts will struggle to continue fermentation at temperatures below 10°C.

Home-brew shops sell electric belts and pads to maintain the temperature of plastic fermentation bins. Neither works entirely satisfactorily because the part of the bin in immediate contact with the belt or pad is raised to a higher temperature than the rest of the liquid. If one is seeking to control the temperature of the must it is better to do so by controlling the temperature of the surrounding air by, for example, fermenting the must in a centrally heated room with the thermostat set at a low level. The domestic ciderist who wishes to create a dedicated cider room or cellar or a cider house in an outbuilding can create an environment in which the temperature and humidity are maintained at predetermined levels by installing cellar conditioning equipment.

THE PROGRESS OF FERMENTATION

At first the continuance of the fermentation will be very obvious because carbon dioxide will continue to bubble at short intervals through the fermentation lock. Towards the end of fermentation the speed of conversion of the sugars reduces and the period between carbon dioxide bubbles being released through the fermentation lock widens so that it becomes difficult to determine, without watching the fermentation lock for a long period whether the fermentation is continuing. At this stage, one might measure the specific gravity of the must at weekly intervals.

As the alcohol level in the must increases and the nutrients are used up yeast cells begin to die and start to sink to the bottom of the fermentation bin forming 'lees'. A complex series of chemical reactions, collectively known as 'autolysis', takes place under which the cells of the yeast are destroyed by their own enzymes. A limited amount of yeast autolysis is beneficial to cider but if the cider is left on its lees for too long the process of autolysis will create unpleasant off-flavours. It is usual, therefore, to rack the cider off the lees after six to eight weeks when the specific gravity will normally have fallen to 1,005 or below. If the fermentation is very slow this first racking might be delayed considerably beyond eight weeks.

TASTING DURING FERMENTATION

Most ciderists will taste their fermenting cider regularly during fermentation to see how it is developing. During fermentation, many ciders develop slightly sulphurous smell reminiscent of rotten eggs, which usually disappear towards the end.

OBTAINING CLARITY

RACKING

Racking not only prevents the development of off-flavours through excessive autolysis, it is also essential to obtain clarity. At the beginning of fermentation, the must will contain many dissolved solids which will gradually come out of the solution and drop to the bottom of the fermentation bin, along with dead yeasts creating lees. When the cider is transferred from one vessel to another it is inevitable that some of this material is stirred up by the process of transfer, so each successive racking leaves most of this matter behind but transfers a little of it with the cider. To achieve a clear, or 'bright' cider, therefore, there must be more than one transfer of the liquid. Clarity is important not just to the appearance of the cider but also to its taste. Excessive suspended yeast in a cider imparts a yeasty taste which some value but most regard as a fault. As noted previously, excessive yeast autolysis will create off-flavours. For all these reasons successive rackings are to be recommended. Each racking, however, will also leave behind some yeast nutrients. That is one reason why the first racking is not undertaken until most of the fermentation has been achieved. Thereafter, the cider should be racked once or twice more before the fully fermented cider is transferred to the maturation vessel. Racking is usually done by siphoning or pumping the cider from one vessel to another empty vessel. If the cider is siphoned, the receiving vessel must be set at a lower level than that of the vessel from which the cider is to be racked.

Top: Racking by siphoning.

Racking with a pump.

HAZINESS

If pectolytic enzyme has been added to the must at the beginning of fermentation and it is racked two or three times before removal to the maturation vessels, it would be extremely unusual for the cider not to be bright and clear. Occasionally, in spite of these procedures, the cider may still be slightly hazy. Clarity can be increased by fining and filtration. Hazes are created when particles in the cider are electrically charged causing them to repel each other so that they do not coalesce to form lumps that fall to the bottom of the must.

FINING

Fining agents are materials which are oppositely charged to the solids commonly suspended in cider and so neutralise their charge, allowing the solids to coalesce and fall to the bottom. Fining is a traditional way of clarifying both wine and cider and in the past fresh blood and egg-white were used. Now mixtures of gelatine and bentonite are used and are available from cider- and winemaking suppliers. Culinary gelatine sold in supermarkets is not of the correct type and should not be used.

FILTRATION

Filtration involves passing the cider through filtration sheets of varying degrees of fineness. It requires an investment in filtration equipment, which is expensive. The problem with filtration is that the sheet filters will also absorb significant amounts of flavour and colour so that the improvement in clarity will be at the cost of flavour and colour. Filtration is rarely used by domestic ciderists.

MATURATION

Once the must's specific gravity has dropped to 998 or below, all – or almost all – of the sugars in the must will have been converted into alcohol and the cider will have fermented to dryness. It will continue to improve with time, however, and so should be stored to allow this process of maturation. Cider can be fermented and drunk within three months of pressing and it will not be unpleasant to taste. For the best results, however, it should not be drunk until at least six months after pressing and nine months is probably the better point at which to broach the previous year's vintage. Saint Swithun's Day or 15 July is a good day to do so. If it is raining on that day, one can console oneself at the prospect of forty days of rain with a restorative glass. If the sun is shining, one can look forward to days of golden sunshine with a glass of golden cider.

During maturation the cider should be kept in vessels that are impermeable to air or nearly so (stainless steel, glass or extra-thick food-grade plastic). These vessels should be fully filled so that there is no head space for air. It is very important, therefore, that the cider should be fully fermented. If it is stored for maturation in closed vessels before all of the sugar has been converted to alcohol, fermentation will continue, carbon dioxide will be released and the storage vessels may explode.

As we have seen, traditionally cider was fermented and stored in unheated buildings or in the open. Fermentation would normally be complete by January or February and the cider would then be stored through the spring until early- to mid-summer. During that time temperatures would rise from near freezing to 20–30°C. Cider houses were often built with thick walls and cellars to reduce the temperature and, just as importantly, to reduce variations in temperature over short periods of time. Captain Silas Taylor read a paper to the Royal Society in 1663 in which he advised that after bottling cider, one should '… lay it in a repository of cool, spring water, two or three foot or more deep.'

Cider, like wine, may be harmed if stored at too high or too low a temperature and by rapid variations in temperature. The ideal temperature for storing cider is probably slightly below that of wine: 10–15°C is ideal with temperatures above freezing and below 20°C being acceptable.

Light promotes various photochemical reactions which are unfavourable to the development of wine. Although experimental evidence that the same is true of cider is lacking, cider is not usually stored in direct sunlight and, if it is stored in glass vessels, it is stored in the dark.

Storing for maturation. It is important that the cider is fully fermented. If the fermentation were to restart, the storage vessels might explode.

MALOLACTIC FERMENTATION

We have already seen that malolactic fermentation can be useful to reduce the acidity of overly acidic cider. Such a fermentation also makes significant changes to flavour. Malolactic fermentation does not involve yeast but a group of bacteria which convert malic acid to lactic acid and carbon dioxide. Such bacteria will be dormant at temperatures of less than approximately 17°C and so, in traditional cidermaking, malolactic fermentation tended to take place in the late spring after alcoholic fermentation was completed and during maturation.

As with alcoholic fermentation, one may rely on naturally occurring (wild) bacteria or use a culture. It is said that malolactic fermentation by wild bacteria gives a spicy taste to cider which cannot be obtained with a culture. There are many different forms of wild bacteria, however, which can have very different effects on taste, not all of them advantageous. The activity of wild bacteria will be inhibited in acidic juices with a pH of 3.6 or less and so, if one desires a malolactic fermentation in order to reduce excessive acidity, one usually uses a malolactic culture. Even malolactic cultures will not ferment at a pH of 3.0 or less. Although malolactic cultures may not impart the spicy flavours which result from malolactic fermentation with wild bacteria, they often produce buttery flavours which are prized by ciderists as well as in the wine industry, particularly in respect of wines made from the Chardonnay grape.

Although carbon dioxide is released in a malolactic fermentation it is highly unlikely that it will be released in a sufficient quantity to burst vessels. Even if cider is bottle conditioned (see Chapter 6) it is unlikely that the carbon dioxide released by the malolactic fermentation in a bottle would have a sufficient effect on the pressure within the bottle to lead to bursts.

After the malolactic fermentation, the active bacteria will die. Unlike the yeasts in alcoholic fermentation, however, the bacteria are so small that they will not leave a significant deposit in the storage vessel.

DISPENSATION

BARRELS AND CASKS

Once the cider has been matured and is ready for drinking it can be transferred to vessels which are convenient for dispensing the cider. Traditionally, cider has been matured in barrels and, when it was ready for drinking, the barrel was broached, a tap inserted and the cider dispensed from the barrel. Alternatively, better-quality cider was bottled once fermentation was completed and dispensed from the bottle.

The trouble with dispensing from the cask, or its modern equivalent the fermentation vessel, is that because such vessels are rigid, as the cider is let out, air is let in. The result will be that the cider remaining in the vessel will deteriorate quickly. One answer is to use storage vessels which have a carbon dioxide injector so that carbon dioxide is released into the vessel to form a blanket over the cider to protect it from air. The difficulty with this is that the pressure of the carbon dioxide ejects the cider with some force from the vessel when the dispensing tap is opened and, particularly when much of the cider has been dispensed, agitates the sediment which, even if the cider has been racked several times before it is dispensed, will have been deposited on the bottom of the vessel.

BAG-IN-BOXES

An alternative is to transfer the cider to 'bag-in-boxes', which are available from a number of home-brew suppliers. These consist of a plastic bag of 5-, 10- or 20-litre capacity with a tap encased in a cardboard box. Because the bag is not rigid, as the cider is dispensed the bag collapses so that no air is admitted into the bag. For short storage periods, these are ideal for dispensing cider. All plastic, however, is to some extent permeable by air and cider should not be stored in bag-in-boxes for more than about ten weeks.

Dispensing from a Manucube.

MANUCUBES

Manucubes are essentially a larger, more robust version of the bag-in-box. Again, they consist of a plastic bag (of 15 litres) to which the cider is transferred when it is ready to be dispensed. The bag is of plastic which is considerably thicker than the plastic used for a bag-in-box. It is placed in a rigid plastic box. Once the bag is filled a tap is added and the cider is ready for dispensing. Because the plastic of the bag is thick, cider in a Manucube will last at least three months and, in my experience, will last perfectly well for six months.

BOTTLES

Glass bottles, either with corks or with crown caps (as are commonly used on beer bottles), are an excellent way of storing cider for dispensation. Cider stored in this way will last for several years.

Cider will only improve with storage for a maximum of two to three years and will deteriorate if it is stored for too long whatever form of storage is used, so bottle storage will certainly keep cider for as long as one is likely to want to keep it. Still cider, however, can be happily stored in its maturation storage vessel until it is ready to be dispensed and then transferred to Manucubes and bags-in-boxes without any deterioration in quality. One might argue, therefore, that storage of still cider in bottles is unnecessarily expensive and time-consuming. Where cider is to be dispensed from a bottle, however, it can be bottled after fermentation and matured in the bottle, thus cutting out one stage of the process.

TASTING

The point of cidermaking is that the cider should be drunk and enjoyed. Producing a cider that tastes good, therefore, is the whole point of the exercise. The ciderist needs to assess the taste of his cider and to endeavour to determine the connections between its final taste and the processes by which it was made. Taste is a fugitive quality, difficult to define. As I have said, whereas well-developed methodologies for tasting wine and describing its taste are widely used, methodologies for tasting and describing cider are not. (For a comprehensive set of taste descriptors see www.cider.org.uk/flavour.htm.)

Attempts to describe and record the taste of cider therefore depend heavily upon the methodology developed for wine. In Appendix 4 I have included an example of a tasting sheet for cider and instructions for using that sheet. It considers separately the qualities of colour, nose and taste and the overall combination of these qualities. The ciderist needs to taste his own cider regularly but also to compare it with other ciders. One needs to remember, however, in tasting commercial cider, that it has to satisfy a wide range of palates and that even commercial ciderists often find themselves forced by their market to produce cider which is sweeter than they would themselves consider to be ideal.

It is important to taste one's cider carefully and to record its qualities.

6: SWEET AND SPARKLING CIDER AND CIDER BRANDY

SWEET CIDER

If one is to make sweet cider one must deal with a fundamental problem. The sweetness of apple juice comes from sugars, primarily fructose. In fermentation, these sugars are converted into alcohol and carbon dioxide. How does one make a sweet cider that is the result of fermentation without restarting that fermentation? There are essentially four approaches. The first is simply to sweeten the cider with sugar and to drink it before the fermentation has had time to restart. The second is to add a sweetener that

A medium-sweet still cider.

is not fermentable by yeast. The third is to kill the yeasts. The fourth and final method is to deliberately create weak yeasts, which will die or become dormant as the alcohol concentration increases and before the must has been fully fermented.

DRINKING BEFORE FERMENTATION RESTARTS

The first approach could be as simple as adding sugar to the cider when it is dispensed into the glass. Alternatively, one could add sugar to the cider at the point at which it is transferred to the dispensing vessel and ensure that it is drunk before it has had a chance to significantly ferment. Where cider has been racked several times and has then been allowed to mature for several months after the cessation of fermentation, even if it begins to 'work' again (that is, to ferment vigorously), it will take some days to do so.

How much sugar is required to achieve any particular level of sweetness? The following table utilises the information given on page 48 to calculate the amount of sugar that should be contained in each litre of cider. If one achieves that by adding sugar, one should, strictly, take account of the increase in the volume of the liquid due to the addition of sugar but in these quantities that increase will be so small as not to make a material difference.

	Sugar (grams per litre)	Specific gravity
Off-dry	10	1,004
Medium dry	20	1,009
Medium sweet	30	1,015
Sweet	40	1,021

Instead of sugar, apple juice can be added, a practice known as 'back sweetening'. The supposed advantage of this is that the apple juice will provide additional flavour to the cider and it is often used where cider is pasteurised (see page 73), as pasteurisation has the effect of reducing the flavour both of apple juice and of cider. The drawback of this method is that apple juice is unlikely to be much more than 15 per cent sugar and so for any degree of sweetening one is going to have to dilute the cider considerably with the apple juice. A compromise is to add a small amount of apple concentrate to the cider. The taste of apple juice is quite different to the taste of cider and so it is not clear why one would wish to mix that flavour with the flavour of one's cider. Back sweetening can provide an interesting variation but it does not seem to me to be a useful general method of sweetening cider.

UNFERMENTABLE SWEETENERS

The second approach of adding an unfermentable sweetener is also quite straightforward. In a way, the addition of a small quantity of pears to the blend to provide sufficient sorbitol to soften the dryness of a fully fermented cider, as discussed in Chapter 3, is an example of this approach. To add an unfermentable sweetener, one simply ferments the cider to dryness and adds sufficient sweetener to achieve the desired level of sweetness. For over a hundred years, saccharin has been used for this purpose and continues to be used by a number of commercial cidermakers. Saccharin, however, has a bitter aftertaste which many find unpleasant. An alternative is the addition of sucralose, an artificial sweetener which has been authorised for use in the European Union in food products since 2004 and in other parts of the world since 1991. Pure sucralose is up to six hundred times sweeter than sugar and twice as sweet as pure saccharin. In a pure form it is difficult for the domestic ciderist to obtain in the small quantities required. It is usually sold in quantities of 100 grams or more, which would be equivalent in sweetness to 60 kg of cane sugar. Because sucralose is so sweet, only tiny amounts are needed to sweeten substantial quantities of cider. For example, to make a medium sweet cider, just 1.5 grams would be required in 30 litres. If pure sucralose is used as a method of sweetening, therefore, the most practical way of measuring out the appropriate amounts is to make up a stock solution by, for example, adding sufficient water to 10 grams of sucralose to create a 1-litre solution, which would then contain 0.1 grams of sucralose to each centilitre.

Alternatively, Splenda is available from most supermarkets and comes in a variety of forms, including tablets which are 11 per cent sucralose with the remainder consisting mainly of bulking ingredients. Each tablet is said to have the sweetening power of a teaspoon of sugar and contains approximately 6 mg of sucralose which would be equivalent to the sweetening power of 3.6 grams of sugar (6 mg x 600).

KILLING YEASTS

Yeast may be reliably destroyed by pasteurisation; that is, by heating. The domestic ciderist will probably pasteurise by placing uncapped bottles of cider in a 'bath' of water. The cider will either have been fermented only so far as to leave the requisite level of residual sugar or it will have been fully fermented and that amount of sugar added which was required for sweetening. For small quantities, the 'bath' might be as simple as a large pan boiled on a stove with a stand placed in the pan to prevent the bottles coming into direct contact with its bottom. For larger quantities, one can buy purpose-built electrically heated units holding large numbers of bottles. The cider is heated to 66°C and then removed from the bath and immediately capped. The temperature of the cider is taken by inserting a thermometer

A small
pasteuriser.

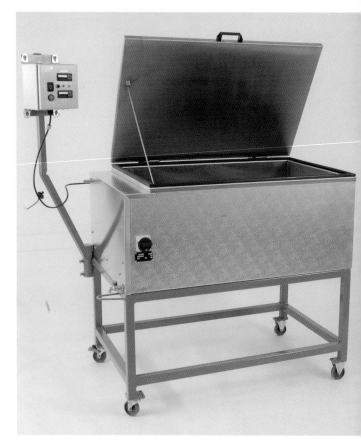

A larger
pasteuriser.

into the open bottle. Having been capped, the bottles are laid on their sides to cool so as to sterilise the top part of the inside of the bottle which had been in contact with the air when the bottle was in the bath.

CREATING WEAK YEASTS

This method relies upon a process of early and repeated racking to reduce the nutrient in the cider and a long maturation to give the yeasts time to die. Yeast nutrient is not added to the must at the beginning of fermentation. At the end of the extended maturation, sugar is added and the cider is stored in cool conditions in the hope that the yeasts will all have died or at least have become dormant to such an extent that they will not be revived by the addition of the small amount of sugar required for sweetening.

An alternative method, if the fermentation sticks at a level of residual sugar which will provide the desired level of sugar, is to rack at that stage to the maturation vessels, being particularly careful to exclude air, and to rely on the weakness of the yeasts due to the low nutrient levels to prevent fermentation restarting. The addition of more sulphite, at half the levels shown in the table on page 59, when the required level of specific gravity is reached may be sufficient to make the fermentation stick at that point. One might, for example, rack when the specific gravity reaches 1,030 and again at 1,025 and then a final time when the target specific gravity is reached, having added sulphite at that point. This additional sulphur dioxide may not become entirely 'bound', so one needs to consider whether the cider will be drunk by those with a sulphur dioxide intolerance.

Either of these two methods is a viable way of producing off-dry cider but, if one wishes to make semi-dry, semi-sweet or sweet cider, the danger is that, if the fermentation does revive, the dispensing vessel (whether it is a bottle, bag-in-box or Manucube) will explode because of the pressure created by the release of carbon dioxide in the revived fermentation. One answer to this problem is to dispense the cider from a pressure barrel. As we have seen, a disadvantage of pressure barrels is that the pressure of the carbon dioxide can force the cider out of the tap when it is opened with such power as to disturb the sediment. An alternative is to store the cider in a vessel fitted with a fermentation lock. It is then transferred to dispensing vessels which are small enough for it to be likely that the cider will be drunk before it has time to 'work' sufficiently to explode the vessels or to deteriorate significantly through air having been drawn into them.

The approach of reducing the nutrient in the juice so as to create weak yeasts which will cease to ferment before complete dryness is reached is the basis of the traditional method of making sweet cider, which is known in Britain as 'keeving' but in France passes under the less appealing name of *défécation*.

Keeving involves the deliberate stimulus of a special sort of pectin gel in which the nutrients in the juice are captured so as to create a must low in nutrients, leading to the development of weak yeasts.

This is done by first deliberately selecting fruit that is low in nutrients. Typically these will be bittersweet cider apples from mature orchards where nitrogenous fertilisers are not used. Table apples, which are high in nutrients, should not be used. The initial sugar level should be high in order to create sufficient alcohol and yet leave enough residual sugar to give the required sweetness. The fruit is milled and pressed at a low temperature. Traditionally this was done simply by storing the fruit until the outside temperature was around 5°C.

When the apples have been milled the pomace is covered and left to stand for up to 24 hours. In winemaking this practice is referred to as *cuvage* or 'maceration' and ciderists have adopted the same terms. The purpose of maceration is to allow pectin to leach out of the apple cells into the must. As the temperature is low, fermentation starts slowly. The pectin is converted into pectic acid by natural pectic esterase enzymes in conjunction with calcium, which are present (in varying amounts) in apple juice, and forms a gel. The pectin gel is partly carried to the surface by the carbon dioxide bubbles released as the fermentation develops, forming a cap, and partly sinks to the bottom. In the process the nutrients in the must are bound into the gel and are therefore concentrated into the lees and the cap. In France the cap is known as the *chapeau brun* but in England and Wales as the 'flying lees'. The must between the lees and the *chapeau brun* has a much lower level of nutrients and yeast than a must undergoing normal fermentation. It is siphoned carefully out of the original fermentation vessel and into another vessel without disturbing the lees or the cap. Fermentation then proceeds normally but will be weak because of the initial low number of yeasts and because of the lack of nutrients.

The drawback of keeving is that it cannot be relied upon to take place If the fruit used happens to have more nutrients or fewer pectins than usual or if the temperature cannot be controlled, then the fermentation may simply proceed normally. So the modern ciderist helps the process. As we have seen the formation of pectate gel requires an enzyme, pectin methyl esterase, and calcium. Additional pectic methyl esterase is added to the must as well as food-grade calcium chloride at a maximum dose of 400 ppm. These additions have not, until recently, been available in quantities appropriate to the domestic ciderist but they may now be obtained under the proprietary label KlerCidre. If the keeving is successful, the fermentation will 'stick' at a specific gravity somewhere between

A *chapeau brun*, or the 'flying lees'.

Conditioned cider brings a smile to your face.

1,020 and 1,010, giving a sweet to medium cider. Keeving may seem to involve a great deal of additional work and a large risk of failure, but many ciderists find the end product worth the additional effort and risk and that making a sweet cider by this method is deeply satisfying.

CONDITIONED CIDER

THE ENGLISH METHOD

The bubbles in sparkling cider or wine are bubbles of carbon dioxide which are absorbed into the liquid when it is kept under pressure in a sealed container (normally a bottle) and are released when the container is opened, the pressure released and the liquid poured into a glass. Conditioned cider is cider where the carbon dioxide is created by a part of the fermentation taking place in the dispensing vessel so that the carbon dioxide released in the fermentation builds up pressure in the vessel. The flavour of the cider is also improved by the autolysis of the small number of yeast cells resulting from this second alcoholic fermentation.

Sparkling industrial cider is made by injecting carbon dioxide into the bottle rather than the creation of carbon dioxide within the bottle. There is nothing wrong with sparkling cider, or wine, which has been carbonated in this way. The bubbles created by conditioning, however, are both smaller and more numerous and the taste of sparkling wine and cider made in this way is fresher, deeper and more complex.

To make bottle-conditioned cider it would be possible to simply bottle one's cider at the point at which its specific gravity indicated that it had the amount of sugar necessary to provide the correct degree of conditioning.

That, however, requires one to measure the specific gravity of every batch constantly to determine the point at which it should be bottled. So it is normal practice to allow the must to ferment to dryness and then to add sugar on bottling. The sugar, in the form of granulated cane sugar, may simply be added to the bottle at bottling, but it will be easier to measure accurately if a solution is made up of sugar and water which is boiled and which can be accurately measured either by using a small culinary measuring-jug or a calibrated pipette.

The amount of sugar required will depend upon the pressure that the type of bottles used can safely withstand. The only types of bottles suitable for bottle conditioning are strong glass bottles designed to take crown caps and, even better than these, strong champagne bottles. Bottle pressure is normally measured in atmospheres or 'bars'. An 800-gram champagne bottle will be safe at 6 atmospheres; a strong crown-capped bottle at 3 atmospheres. The addition of 10 grams of sugar per litre will create a pressure of 3 atmospheres, whereas 20 grams per litre will create a pressure of 6 atmospheres. It is important that the cider should be completely fermented before it is bottled and that the added sugar is measured precisely for, if the cider contains too much sugar on bottling, the bottles may explode.

The yeast remaining in suspension in the cider will normally be sufficient for the fermentation to restart. Some ciderists add additional yeast nutrient at this stage and some will even add additional yeast. Personally, I have never experienced a bottle where fermentation has not restarted and so rather than adding the yeast or yeast nutrient I would simply take the risk that the fermentation will not restart. After all, if that is the case, one will simply have a pleasant off-dry or medium-dry still cider.

It will help the fermentation if the bottles are stored initially at the top end of the range for storage temperatures at, say, 15–18°C.

It is possible to use vessels other than bottles, such as a keg, for conditioned cider. The trouble is that if all of the cider is not to be consumed at the same time so that some of the cider is left in the cask, air will be drawn into the cask leading to a rapid oxidation and deterioration of the cider. In theory it would be possible to inject carbon dioxide to maintain the pressure. To do so, however, would be to lose the advantage of conditioning over carbonation. In any event, I have never been able to obtain a keg capable of maintaining sufficient pressure. Beer kegs have pressure-release valves normally designed to release pressure at a lower level than the pressure necessary for satisfactory carbonation.

One of the drawbacks of conditioning in a bottle is that the multiplication and subsequent death of the yeast in the fermentation process throws a deposit, so that the cider must be allowed to rest upright for some hours before pouring and must be poured very carefully. Even then, the last inch of cider in the bottle will inevitably be slightly cloudy and in order to preserve brightness should be drunk separately from the rest of the cider in the bottle. The French solved this problem by the introduction of *remuage* and *dégorgement* in the nineteenth century. This involves gradually inverting the bottles during the process of maturation in the bottle so that the yeast deposit settles in the neck (*remuage*), freezing the yeast deposit by inserting the neck of the bottle in a mixture of ice and salt (because the freezing point of the mixture is lower than that of ice on its own) and then opening the bottle so that the accumulated pressure expels the frozen plug of deposit (*dégorgement*). The bottle is then quickly topped up and a new cork wired into the bottle. In the commercial production of champagne this process is now largely automated. The use of a cultured champagne yeast helps the process, for such yeasts have been designed to be especially 'flocculent' – that is, to form easily into clumps so that they naturally form a plug in the neck of the bottle.

Remuage and *dégorgement* are skilful processes which require some practice but this method can result in the very best cider which is made. Certainly, if I had to recommend a single commercial cider as showing cider at its best it would be a cider made using this method, by a well-known Somersetshire producer.

SPARKLING SWEET CIDER

Because bottle conditioning requires fermentation in the bottle, it is very difficult to make sweet cider in this way. It is occasionally done by opening bottles at regular intervals to test their specific gravity and then pasteurising the remaining bottles when the required specific gravity is reached. Any opened bottle, of course, will have lost its pressure so the method is only suitable when a large number of bottles are to be made. It also depends on the assumption that the untested bottles of sweet cider are fermenting at the same rate as those which are tested.

The normal method of making sparkling sweet cider, therefore, even for ciderists, is by carbonation of pasteurised cider, requiring the purchase of equipment for carbon dioxide injection.

CIDER BRANDY

EVAPORATIVE DISTILLATION

The first recorded reference to the evaporative distillation of spirits from cider is in 1553 when Gilles de Gouberville installed an alembic still at his manor in Mesnil-au-Val on the Cotentin Peninsula. In 1684, Sir Richard Haines was granted a monopoly in the distillation of cider by Charles II. Cider distillation grew into a large industry in France, particularly in Calvados in Normandy which is now a protected designation. It failed to do so in England and today only a handful of licensed producers of cider brandy operate in the United Kingdom.

Evaporative distillation takes advantage of the fact that ethyl alcohol has a different boiling point (78.4°C) from water (100°C) and other liquids found in alcoholic solutions. By heating a liquid to various temperatures one boils off different liquids within it which can then be liquefied again by cooling so as to separate the alcohol from the other liquids. Although it is true that if one mistook a liquid resulting from boiling at one temperature for the ethyl alcohol which would be obtained from boiling at another, one could drink a number of liquids that are harmful in concentration, it is nevertheless a straightforward matter, with the correct equipment, to produce a drinkable spirit from cider. Unfortunately, it is against the law in the United Kingdom (and in the United States) to produce spirits without a licence. In practice, licences are not issued in the United Kingdom to individuals who wish to establish stills to make spirits for home consumption. Even if issued with a licence, the domestic cider brandy maker would have to pay excise duty on the cider brandy he produced for his own consumption! This may be contrasted with the production of cider itself which is unregulated by the state in the United Kingdom provided it is not offered for sale. Why it is necessary for the state to interfere in the private activities of individuals in this way is not obvious, except that doing so makes it easier for the government to collect the excise duties it exacts on the production of spirits.

Although the production of spirits without a licence is illegal in the United Kingdom, the sale and purchase of stills for evaporative distillation is not and the purchaser does not require a licence to possess one. Stills are available from several suppliers of cidermaking equipment.

The cider brandy produced by the leading licensed producer (see Appendix 6) is at least the equal of the best calvados. The ciderist, frustrated by a legal prohibition preventing him from making his own cider brandy, can at least console himself by tasting a commercial product that demonstrates how good cider brandy can be.

A copper-pot still.

FREEZE DISTILLATION AND APPLEJACK

In Canada and the northern parts of the United States there is a long tradition of making 'applejack' from cider. Applejack concentrates the alcohol in cider by freez-

The Somerset
Cider Brandy
Company Ltd's
still.

distillation – the opposite process to evaporative distillation. It takes
advantage of the fact that alcohol has a lower freezing point than water so
that the water is frozen and the unfrozen alcohol is tapped off.
Unfortunately, the aldehydes and esters which in evaporative distillation are
separated in the 'heads' and the fusel oils which are separated in the 'tails'
remain, in freeze distillation, in the unfrozen liquid. This explains why
applejack is notorious for giving particularly strong hangovers. As we
have already seen, the production of spirits in the United Kingdom
and the United States is illegal without a licence, regardless of the method
of production.

7: COMPETITIONS, WASSAILS, FÊTES, RAFFLES AND SALES

COMPETITIONS

Having made one's cider and achieved a result with which one is satisfied it is natural to wonder how one's efforts compare with others. A number of cider competitions are run at country shows (see Appendix 6 for details). At the minimum they will normally have classes for dry, medium and sweet cider. They are usually inexpensive to enter and the normal format is for the entrant to provide either one or two bottles or demijohns of cider before the start of judging. If there is a sparkling cider class, one is normally required to provide an entry in a wired champagne-type bottle. It is rare for such competitions to publish the criteria by which the cider is to be judged. Quite often, they do not even provide definitions of the competition classes or even of what constitutes 'cider'.

It is said that the judges tend to look for cider of the type made in the traditional cidermaking areas – that is, a cider made from cider apples and with high tannin levels. Like all competitive events, to be enjoyable the competitions need to be taken seriously but with a sense of proportion. It really is not the winning, but the taking part that matters.

WASSAILS

The English word 'wassail' derives (via Anglo-Saxon) from the Old Norse 'ves heill', meaning 'be in good health', and refers to a large number of ancient customs of hospitality to neighbours and friends in the Christmas season and in particular to the drinking of toasts. In the traditional cidermaking areas wassailing takes a very particular form in which cider toasts are drunk in the orchard, toasted bread is offered to the spirit of the apple trees, loud noises are made and guns are fired to scare away evil spirits from the trees.

In recent years many surviving orchard wassails have been revived and some have even been instituted for the first time. Villages such as the Somersetshire villages of Drayton (5 January) and Carhampton (17 January) and Bodmin in Cornwall (6 January) hold wassails, as do many individual cidermakers.

The dates on which wassails take place reflect a common confusion over the date of Twelfth Night. The liturgical season of Christmas begins on Christmas Day and so Twelfth Night is the night of 5 January. Many wassails, however, are celebrated on the night of 6 January. To confuse things even further some are celebrated on the day Twelfth Night would have been had the Gregorian calendar not been adopted. When the Gregorian calendar was adopted in 1752 the date was adjusted by eleven days to compensate for the cumulative effect of the discrepancy between the Julian calendar and the period of the Earth's orbit around the sun. Some of those who insist on the Julian date, however, add eleven days to 5 January, holding the wassail on 17 January rather than on 16 January. Whether the wassail is held on 5, 6, 16 or 17 January, it is a pleasant opportunity for people to come together on a bleak January night, to have a little fun and to enjoy drinking good cider.

A cider competition held at Long Ashton on 7 May 1936.

Wassailing in the
1950s.

FÊTES AND RAFFLES

Cidermaking is a sociable activity and ciderists like to see their cider bein
drunk by their family, friends and neighbours. They may want to donate the
cider to public events such as church outings, village fêtes or other events fc
free consumption at the event, to be sold or to be offered as prizes i
competitions. It may be that in a year of high production they will want t
sell their surplus cider. How does the law affect all of this?

LICENSING OF PREMISES

First, any premises from which alcoholic drinks are sold for consumption b
the public must either be licensed or the event must be subject to
temporary event notice.[1] Obtaining a full premises licence is a majc
operation only suitable for those conducting a substantial business of sellir
alcohol to the public. A temporary event notice may be given by the premise
user in respect of a proposed event with fewer than 500 attendees.[2] Th
notice must be given (together with payment of a small fee) at least te
working days before the event [3] and a copy of it must be sent to the police.
The event is not authorised until the Local Authority has acknowledge
receipt.[5] The Authority has a duty to do so by the end of the working da

following receipt (if it is received on a working day).[6] There are provisions allowing for objection by the police or Local Authority.[7] An individual who does not hold a personal licence to sell alcohol may give up to five temporary event notices per year,[8] and one who does may give up to fifty temporary event notices per year.[9] Personal licences are intended for persons who are conducting substantial business activities.

REGISTRATION UNDER THE FOOD HYGIENE REGULATIONS

In addition, any food business operator must register with the Local Authority.[10] A food business is 'any undertaking, whether for profit or not and whether public or private, carrying out any of the activities related to any stage of production, processing or distribution of food.'[11] Such activities do not include '… primary production for private domestic use or … the domestic preparation, handling or storage of food for private domestic consumption.'[12] 'Food' for this purpose includes drinks.[13]

REGISTRATION WITH HMRC

Excise duty is charged on all cider brought into the United Kingdom or made in the United Kingdom by a person who is required to be registered as a maker of cider.[14] Any person who, in any premises in the United Kingdom, makes cider for sale must be registered with Her Majesty's Revenue and Customs in respect of those premises.[15] The duty is charged at a fixed rate per hectolitre. There are three different rates, according to the alcoholic strength of the cider.[16]

A cidermaker who is otherwise liable to registration under s.62(2) is exempt from the requirement to register if he makes a claim to that effect and his 'production of cider does not exceed seventy hectolitres in a period of twelve consecutive months.'[17] A person who claims exemption under this

---

6 Licensing Act 2003 s.1
7 Licensing Act 2003 s.100(5)(d)
8 Licensing Act 2003 s.100(7)
9 Licensing Act 2003 s.104
5 Licensing Act 2003 s.102
6 Licensing Act 2003 s.102(1)
7 Licensing Act 2003 ss.104–107
8 Licensing Act 2003 s.107(2)
9 Licensing Act 2003 s.107(3)
0 EU Regulation 852/2004 Article 6(2)
1 EU Regulation 178/2002 Article 3(2)
2 EU Regulation 178/2002 Article 1(3)
3 EU Regulation 178/2002 Article 2
4 Alcoholic Liquor Duties Act 1979 s.62(1)
5 Alcoholic Liquor Duties Act 1979 s.62(2)
6 Alcoholic Liquor Duties Act 1979 s.62(1A)
7 Cider and Perry (Exemption from Registration) Order 1976 paragraph 2

'Small Cidermaker's Exemption' must 'furnish to the Commissioners on request such records of or information about his production of cider as may be necessary to establish that the conditions of [the exemption] are or have been complied with.'

Cider for the purposes of Excise Duty has a special definition:[18]

> Cider (or perry) –
> (a) which is of a strength exceeding 1.2 per cent but less than 8.5 per cent,
> (b) which is obtained from the fermentation of apple or pear juice, without the addition at any time of –
>   (i)   any alcoholic liquor, or
>   (ii) any liquor or substance which communicates colour or flavour, other than such as the Commissioners may allow as appearing to them to be necessary to make cider (or perry),
> (c) the pre-fermentation mixture for which satisfies the pre-fermentation juice requirement, and
> (d) which satisfies the final product juice requirement.

The pre-fermentation juice requirement and the final product juice requirement are designed to ensure that to be cider a liquor must have been made from ingredients which are at least 35 per cent apple and/or pear juice.

Cider for this purpose also does not include cider that is sold in packages or with accompanying documentation which states that its alcoholic content is 8.5 per cent or more, whether it is or not.[19]

It can be seen that not all cider falls within the meaning of cider for the purposes of the duties on cider. If it does not, it will fall within the definition of 'made wine'.[20] Made wine bears duty at a higher rate than 'cider' and the Small Cidermaker's Exemption does not apply to it. The special definition of cider can be a trap for the domestic ciderist selling small amounts of his surplus production, as we shall see.

GIVING CIDER TO THE ORGANISERS OF AN EVENT

If one merely gives cider to the organisers of an event, one neither has to charge duty on the cider nor does one require a temporary event notice. The organisers of the event, however, if the charge for admission includes the right to be served alcoholic refreshment or if they sell alcoholic liquor or i

---

18 Alcoholic Liquor Duties Act 1979 s.1(6) and the Alcoholic Liquor Duties (Definition of Cider) Order 2010 Article 21 (with effect where fermentation starts on or after 1 September 2010)
19 Alcoholic Liquor Duties Act 1979 s.55B
20 Alcoholic Liquor Duties Act 1979 s.1(5)

is offered as a prize in a competition where the entrant pays money in order to take part, will require either a full premises licence or to have given a temporary event notice.

It is arguable that the donor is a 'food business operator' for the purpose of the Food Hygiene Regulations and therefore ought to register with the Local Authority. One might argue, however, that his activity does not amount to an 'undertaking'. Undertaking is a word of wide meaning, but, probably, is not wide enough to cover the simple making of cider for one's own consumption and for gifts. It may be that in practice the Local Authority will not enforce the duty to register in such circumstances, but the safe course of action is to contact the Authority and to explain the circumstances.

SELLING ONE'S SURPLUS CIDER

If a ciderist sells his surplus production he will not require either a premises licence or be required to give a temporary event notice provided the person to whom he is selling it is not a member of the public. He will have a duty to register with the Local Authority as a food business operator. He must either register with HMRC or, if all of the cider he produces is cider within the special definition and his scale of production falls within the Small Cidermaker's Exemption, he must make a claim for that exemption.[21] It does not appear from the regulations that he has to make the claim in advance of making the sale. He needs to pay careful attention to the special definition of cider. If, for example, his cider were 8.5 per cent alcohol or more, or he had added some juice of a fruit other than pear to his must, or he had added honey instead of sugar to increase the alcoholic content, his cider would be 'made wine' for the purposes of excise duty. He would then be required to register with HMRC and to pay duty in respect of all of the cider that he had made, including the cider which he consumed himself.[22]

---

21 This is subject to one interesting point. The duty to be registered applies to a person who 'makes cider for sale'. The use of the word 'for' implies purpose. If the cider is made with the intention of it being consumed domestically and that intention is subsequently changed, it would appear that there is no duty to register. It appears that HMRC do not accept that this is the case.

22 Cider and Perry Regulations 1989 paragraph 12A. He could, however, make an application under Cider and Perry Regulations 1989 para 24 to be relieved from duty on the cider which he consumes himself.

APPENDIX 1: GLOSSARY

ABV (Alcohol by volume) A measure of the alcoholic content of a beverage expressed as the percentage by volume of alcohol in the beverage.

Acetification The process whereby alcohol is oxidised to form acetic acid.

Aerobic fermentation Fermentation by yeasts requiring oxygen from the air.

Anaerobic fermentation Fermentation by yeasts requiring only oxygen from the fermenting must itself.

Autolysis The breaking down of dead yeast cells from contact with a fermented liquid.

Back sweetening Sweetening cider by adding apple juice or apple concentrate after fermentation has stopped.

Bag-in-box A dispensing vessel consisting of an inner plastic bag placed in a cardboard box.

Bentonite Diatomaceous clay used as a fining agent.

Beverage Ciderkin or small cider (now archaic).

Bittersharp A classification of cider apples having more than 0.45 per cent acid and 0.2 per cent tannin.

Bittersweet A classification of cider apples having not more than 0.45 per cent acid and more than 0.2 per cent tannin.

Bright Cider that is clear.

Campden tablet A proprietary tablet containing a measured amount of sodium metabisulphite sufficient to give 50 ppm of sulphur dioxide when dissolved in 1 gallon of liquid.

Carbonation The injection of carbon dioxide into a liquid under pressure.

Chapeau brun The French term for the brown cap that forms on cider during keeving.

Chaptalisation The French term for adding sugar to wine during fermentation to increase its alcohol content. Named after Jean-Antoine Chaptal, Comte de Chanteloup (1756–1832). The term is often used by British ciderists.

Cheese A pile of layers (or hairs) of apple pomace where each layer is wrapped in a cloth and separated by a rack in preparation for pressing.

Cider apple An apple of a cultivar recognised as particularly suitable for making cider.

Cider brandy Distilled liquor of cider.

Cider sickness A condition under which cider forms a milky haze.

Ciderkin Cider with a weak alcoholic strength, typically of less than 4.5 per cent alcohol, usually resulting from a second pressing of pomace (see 'Small cider').

Completely dry A drink in which all the original sugar has been fermented into alcohol.

Conditioned Cider which has been partially fermented in a sealed vessel such as a bottle with the result that on the vessel being opened the cider releases carbon dioxide bubbles.

Craft cider Cider made aimed at being of the highest quality practicable.

Culinary apple An apple from a cultivar suitable for use in cooking.

Cultivar All trees grown by propagation from a particular tree with recognised qualities.

Cuvage The practice of leaving the pomace for a period, normally of twenty-four hours, before pressing it to promote the production of pectin and changes in tannins.

Cyser Cider strengthened with honey before fermentation.

Défécation The French term for keeving.

Dégorgement A technique for removing the yeast deposit from bottle-conditioned wine or cider by freezing the deposit in the bottle's neck and releasing its closure for the period of time necessary for the pressure in the bottle to expel the deposit.

Demijohn A jar made of thick glass, normally of 1-gallon capacity, with an aperture designed to take a bung.

Devonshire colic A disease common in eighteenth-century Devonshire, caused by lead in the equipment then used for cidermaking.

Domestic ciderist A ciderist whose cider is not produced for sale.

Dry A description of a drink in which all, or nearly all, of the original sugar has been fermented into alcohol.

Ethanol/Ethyl alcohol A colourless, volatile, flammable liquid alcohol present in alcoholic drinks.

Feints A generic term for the heads and tails of cider brandy distillation which are put aside to be re-distilled.

Fermentation A biochemical process of the nature of that involved in the action of yeast on sugars or dough, involving effervescent evolution of heat and chemical breakdown of the substance acted on.

Filtration The passing of a liquid through a barrier to remove particles.

Fining Treating a liquid with a material that attracts solids as it passes through the liquid so as to clarify the liquid.

Flying lees The English term for the cap that forms during keeving.

Fully fermented An alcoholic liquid in which all of the fermentable sugar has been converted into ethyl alcohol and carbon dioxide.

Hair A layer of pomace in a 'cheese'.

Hard tannin Tannin which imparts a bitter and astringent flavour.

HDPE (High Density Polyethylene) A high-quality plastic used with food and drink, among other uses.

Heads Substances with a boiling point less than ethyl alcohol, which are first boiled off in the process of evaporative distillation.

Hydrometer An instrument for measuring the specific gravity of a liquid.

Inoculum A cultured yeast added to a must.

Keeving A traditional cidermaking technique for making sweet cider.

Lactic acid An acid commonly found in milk and yoghurt, which results from malolactic fermentation.

Lag phase of fermentation The first stage of alcoholic fermentation, i.e. the period between the juice being pressed (or, when cultured yeasts are used, the cultured yeast being added to the must) and the first visible signs of fermentation.

Lees Dead yeast and other solids that fall out of the solution in a must.

Maceration The practice of leaving the pomace for a period, normally of twenty-four hours, before pressing it, to promote the production of pectin and changes in tannins.

Malic acid The principal acid found in apples, usually constituting 90 per cent of the total acid content.

Malolactic fermentation A fermentation not involving yeasts whereby malic acid is converted into lactic acid and carbon dioxide.

Malus pumila The domestic table apple, probably introduced by the Romans into Britain.

Malus sieversii The apple from which all domestic apples are descended, found in the Tienshan Mountains in Kazakhstan.

Malus sylvestris The true common crab apple indigenous to Britain.

Manucube A dispensing vessel consisting of a robust inner plastic bag placed in a rigid plastic box.

Maturation The process of benign chemical change taking place when cider is stored after fermentation in correct conditions.

Mill A mechanical device for chopping apples into smaller pieces to form the pomace in preparation for its being pressed in cidermaking.

Mouse A condition in which cider develops a taste said to be reminiscent of the smell of the male mouse, making the cider unpalatable.

Must Pressed juice prepared for fermentation.

Oxidation Chemical reactions caused by contact with oxygen.

Pasteurisation The destruction of micro-organisms by heating in order to prevent spoilage.

Pectin Natural carbohydrates found in apples and many other fruits, responsible for forming gels and hazes in cider.

Pectolytic enzyme An enzyme normally added to the must at the start of fermentation with the purpose of preventing the formation of pectin hazes.

Perry A drink made by fermenting pear juice.

Perry pears Pears of cultivars recognised as being particularly suitable for the making of perry.

Pomace Apples milled or scratted in preparation for pressing.

Potassium metabisulphite A sterilising chemical containing sulphur dioxide in the form of a potassium salt, used both in sterilising cidermaking equipment and as a sterilant in apple juice, must and cider.

Potential final alcohol The amount of alcohol that will be contained in a cider if the must from which it is made is fully fermented.

ppm (parts per million) The proportion of a substance in a liquid expressed in millionths.

ppt (parts per thousand) The proportion of a substance in a liquid expressed in thousandths.

Press A mechanical device for pressing apples.

Press cloth A cloth, now usually made from terylene, nylon or other polyester, which is used to wrap the apple pomace for pressing in a rack and cloth press.

Primary phase of fermentation The second stage of alcoholic fermentation when a vigorous fermentation is established, creating a froth on the surface of the must.

Quinic acid An acid found in apples, typically constituting 10 per cent of the total acid.

Racking Transferring cider from one vessel to another while leaving the lees behind.

Remuage The French term for the technique of gradually moving and twisting bottles of sparkling wine or cider in order to move their lees to the neck preparatory to *dégorgement*.

Riddling The English term for the technique of gradually moving and twisting bottles of sparkling wine or cider in order to move their lees to the neck preparatory to *dégorgement*.

Rootstock The root system and stem of a tree onto which a scion is grafted in tree propagation.

Scion A shoot or twig cut for grafting in tree propagation.

Scratter A type of mill with contra-rotating interlocking drums with blunt teeth, which roughly breaks up apples prior to pressing. When of the size used by domestic ciderists they are normally manually operated.

Scrumpy Rough, strong cider made in the traditional cidermaking areas of the West Country mainly for home consumption and sale to passing trade.

Secondary phase of fermentation The third stage of alcoholic fermentation when the froth created by the primary phase of fermentation has subsided.

Seedling A tree that has grown from seed rather than from a graft.

Sharp A classification of cider apples having more than 0.45 per cent acid and not more than 0.2 per cent tannin.

Small cider Cider with a weak alcoholic strength, typically of less than 4.5 per cent alcohol, usually resulting from a second pressing of pomace (see 'Ciderkin').

Sodium metabisulphite A sterilising chemical containing sulphur dioxide in the form of a sodium salt, used both in sterilising cidermaking equipment and as a sterilant in apple juice, must and cider.

Soft tannin Tannin which imparts a bitter and mildly astringent flavour.

Sorbitol An unfermentable sugar found in pears.

Specific gravity The ratio of the density of a substance to the density of a given reference material; in particular, a measure of the density of a liquid by reference to a scale on which distilled water is 1,000. The measure is used to determine the sugar content of a must and to estimate potential final alcohol.

Spent (or dry) pomace Pomace which has been pressed.

Sticking Occurs, in respect of fermentation, when fermentation ceases before the must has been fermented to dryness.

Still (1) Cider or wine which does not release any carbon dioxide bubbles – one which does not sparkle.

Still (2) An apparatus used for evaporative distillation of liquids.

Sulphiting Adding sulphur dioxide in the form of potassium or sodium metabisulphite to a juice, must or cider.

Sweet A classification of cider apples having not more than 0.45 per cent acid and not more than 0.2 per cent tannin.

Table apple An apple recognised as suitable for eating without cooking.

Tails Substances, mainly fusel oils, with a boiling point higher than alcohol but less than water which are boiled off during evaporative distillation.

Taint The spoilage of cider by picking up trace flavours, usually from unclean vessels.

Tannin A diversely complex group of chemical compounds found in many fruits, including apples, which have the capability of interacting with proteins so as to increase their molecular size. They play an important part in determining the flavour of cider, its depth, complexity and body. Tannins impart a bitter and astringent feel in the mouth.

Wilding A tree grown from seed and not by deliberate human choice.

Working Vigorous fermentation especially in the primary phase of fermentation.

Yeast Micro-organisms responsible for fermentation.

Yeast nutrients Chemicals on which yeast 'feeds', principally thiamine and amino acids. They are naturally present in apple juice to some degree but are often added to musts in a powdered form.

APPENDIX 2:
TROUBLESHOOTING

Acetification is the process by which vinegar is produced from ethyl alcohol. It results from the multiplication of *Acetobacter* bacteria which are present in apple juice and will multiply if the juice is exposed to the air forming sheets of brown jelly on the surface of the cider. The first symptom of acetification will be a rise in acidity but once it has begun to develop it can be detected from the smell of vinegar. If acetification develops it will almost always be after fermentation is finished because the release of carbon dioxide during fermentation will both prevent the must from coming into contact with air and will stop the jelly coalescing.

Keeping the cider well insulated from air should prevent the fault from developing. Once it has developed, its further development can be stopped by pasteurisation. Small amounts of acetification can be neutralised by the addition of potassium carbonate. If, however, the condition has progressed very far there will be nothing to do but allow the cider to turn to cider vinegar. If one decides to do this, the temperature of the acetified cider must be kept at around 20°C. It should also be kept entirely separate from the rest of one's cidermaking operation and the vessel thoroughly scrubbed and cleaned after use. Alternatively, one may simply wish to discard the acetified cider and be careful in future to exclude air from contact with the must.

Blackening and greening Discoloration of ciders will often be caused by contact with metal. It is, therefore, of the utmost importance to avoid any contact between any metals other than stainless steel, and the apples, pomace, must and cider. Although the process of metallic discoloration includes oxidation being catalysed by the metal, metallic discoloration is not to be confused with the darkening which results from simple oxidation.

Contact with copper will give a green colour to the cider. Copper will also taint the flavour of the cider. Once the condition has developed there is little one can do.

Contact with iron will lead to blackening. The traditional remedy was to add fresh wheat bran to the cider (at 1.5 grams per litre). The bran trapped the metals and then settled at the bottom of the fermentation vessel. The cider was then racked off to another vessel. This practice may solve the problem in some cases.

Cider sickness is characterised by a milky haze and a smell of rotten bananas or lemons. It occurs when acetaldehyde is produced which unites with the tannins in the must. It may well disappear after several months but it will have resulted in the destruction of the tannins, and the cider will develop a weak and insipid flavour. The bacteria which cause the creation of acetaldehyde cannot survive in solutions which have a pH of 3.6 or less and so the condition is unlikely to develop if one has adjusted the acidity of the must at the beginning of fermentation. The condition can be arrested by the addition of malic acid until the pH is below 3.7.

Film yeasts form a greasy film on the surface of the cider which looks rather like ash. Again, they are unlikely to develop if the must is protected from contact with the air, particularly if it has been sulphited. Further development of the fault can be stopped by the addition of sulphite (to a maximum of 100 ppm) and by the exclusion of air. The effect of the film yeast is to impart to the cider a smell like a cross between nail varnish remover and vinegar and, sometimes, a musky or oxidised flavour. If the development is stopped before the problem has developed too far the cider is likely to remain drinkable, if less good than it otherwise would have been. If the cider is racked, the film already formed on the surface may be left behind on the side of the fermentation vessel, although that will not remove the effect which it has already had on the cider's flavour.

Mousiness Cider can develop a taste which some describe as being like the smell of the male mouse. The reasons for its development are complicated but it is prevented by the exclusion of oxygen from the must and it is less likely to develop if the must is sulphited. There is no remedy once the condition has developed.

Ropinesss, oiliness and thickness These conditions are caused by anaerobic lactic acid bacteria and are most often found in insufficiently acidic ciders, particularly those which have not been racked from their lees. Flavour is little affected but they result in the cider pouring, in the early stages, like light oil and, in the later stages, in slimy ropes with a consistency of cooked egg-white. They will not generally occur in ciders with sufficient acidity, particularly if they have been sulphited. It may be possible to break up the gel by stirring the vessel well and adding sodium metabisulphite. Fining may also be of help.

Sulphur smells In the early stages of fermentation cider will often develop a smell slightly reminiscent of rotten eggs. Provided it is not too pronounced it will usually clear of its own accord during fermentation. If the smell is very strong during fermentation or if it does not clear during it, it is probably caused by excess hydrogen sulphide or some related compound. Excess hydrogen sulphide can be neutralised with copper. One can test if excess hydrogen sulphide is indeed the cause, by taking a small sample of the offending cider and placing a copper object in it. If the aroma has decreased after a quarter of an hour it will have been caused by excess hydrogen sulphide. In that case the addition of copper sulphate in extremely small quantities will cure the condition.

APPENDIX 3: EQUIPMENT

This section lists the equipment that one is likely to require in one's first year as a ciderist. I give two lists. The first is for someone intending to make only 50 litres of cider and wishing to keep down his costs until he is sure he is going to make cider annually. The second is for a person who intends to make 200 litres of cider and who is willing to make a capital investment because he is confident that he will wish to make cider for the foreseeable future. The former will require something in the region of 100 kg of apples because his basket press is unlikely to be more than 50 per cent efficient. The latter will require about 300 kg of apples if his hydropress achieves an efficiency of 66.67 per cent.

For other volumes of cider up to 200 litres, List 1 could be adjusted proportionately for items such as fermentation bins, the required quantity of which will vary with volume. For 100 litres but less than 200 litres I would recommend that a 36-litre crossbeam press or a small hydropress is bought, as well as a manual scratter or electric mill. For volumes of cider of more than 200 litres, many of the items in List 2 will require larger quantities. For volumes of 500 litres or more I would recommend a 90-litre hydropress.

Not all of the items will be needed in the early stages of the process from harvest to the beginning of fermentation. For example, the larger-scale ciderist will need half of the fermenters when the cider is racked towards the end of fermentation and half at the next racking. There may be some other items required depending upon the progress of cidermaking. For example, it may be that the ciderist will also have to buy sugar if he intends to supplement the natural sugar in the juice; and if he has to supplement the acidity of the juice he might have to buy malic acid. It is assumed that he is not attempting a cultured malolactic fermentation. If he wishes to bottle some of his cider he will need bottles and closures and a suitable bottle-brush.

LIST 1:
- Robust bucket of food-grade plastic of 25-litre capacity
- Substantial length of timber of 10cm^2 section
- 20-litre crossbeam press
- Packet of cotton-wool balls
- Plastic or stainless-steel strainer
- Two food-grade bowls (suitable for use as washing-up bowls)
- Food-grade plastic funnel
- Glass measuring-jug
- Washing-up brush
- Three 25-litre fermenters made of food-grade plastic with airlocks
- Three 1-gallon demijohns
- Three airlocks for demijohns

- Three rubber bungs for demijohns
- Siphon tube with U-bend
- Hydrometer
- Hydrometer jar
- Twenty pH strips
- 1 kg sodium metabisulphite
- One drum (100) Campden tablets
- 100 grams yeast nutrient
- 25 grams pectolase
- Cultured yeast sufficient for 60 litres of cider
- Five 10-litre bag-in-boxes
- Jar of Vaseline

LIST 2:

- Two tarpaulins
- Thirty vented plastic stacking containers (each capable of holding 10 kg of apples)
- Electric mill
- A 40-litre hydropress with straining bag
- Packet of cotton-wool balls
- Plastic sieve
- Two food-grade bowls (suitable for use as washing-up bowls)
- Food-grade plastic funnel
- Glass measuring-jug
- Washing-up brush
- Twelve 30-litre fermenters made of extra-thick food-grade plastic with airlocks and closers
- Eight 1-gallon demijohns
- Eight airlocks for demijohns
- Eight rubber bungs for demijohns
- Three siphon tubes with U-bends
- Thermometer
- Hydrometer
- Hydrometer jar
- Electronic pH meter
- Titration kit
- 2 kg sodium metabisulphite
- 1 drum (100) Campden tablets
- 300 grams yeast nutrient
- Jar of Vaseline
- 100 grams pectolase
- Cultured yeast sufficient for 210 litres of cider
- Five Manucubes and bags

APPENDIX 4:
TASTING METHODOLOGY

The tasting sheets which follow can be used for recording the impressions a cider makes on you when tasted. If you contact the author on rudgecidermaker1@yahoo.co.uk he will endeavour to send an electronic version of the tasting sheets to you. There follows guidance on completing the testing sheets.

BASIC INFORMATION

Page 1 records the basic information about the cider. With commercial cider most of this information will be available on the label of the bottle. The region will be the country, and region of that country, where the cider was made. In respect of cider made in Britain the county should also be given if possible (for example: England, the West Country, Somersetshire). Note: sparkling/still – 'Y' indicates that the cider is sparkling; 'N' indicates that the cider is still.

COLOUR

Limpidity is the clarity of the cider. Please grade it 1–5 with 5 indicating a crystal-clear cider and 1 a cloudy cider.

Brilliance is the brightness of the cider. Mark it 1–5 with 5 being a dazzling cider and 1 a murky cider.

Intensity is the depth of the colour. Grade the cider 1–5 with 5 being a deep colour and 1 a pale colour.

Tint is the colour of the cider. Please use the following descriptions giving the number in Tint (No.) and the description in Tint (Description). If you find that none of these colours adequately describe the cider use some additional description but do not substitute your description for the numbered categories given:

1. White yellow
2. Pale yellow
3. Light yellow
4. Straw
5. Canary
6. Gold
7. Amber
8. Old gold
9. Orange

NOSE

'Nose' is the name for the smell of the cider. Alternative terms are 'aroma', usually used of young ciders, and 'bouquet', usually used for mature ciders.

Intensity is the strength of the smell of the cider. Please grade this 1–5 with 1 being a light nose and 5 a very strong one.

Aromatic nuances Place the cider in one of the following categories:

1. Floral
2. Dried and crystallised fruits
3. Earthy scents
4. Food products
5. Balsamic
6. Spices
7. Fresh fruits
8. Plant scents
9. Animal scents
10. Minerals
11. Woody

You may use more than one of these category headings because it is quite possible for ciders to remind you, for example, of a flavour and a spice. If exceptionally, you do not think it comes into any of these categories, leave blank and complete the aromatic nuances (description) box. In that box you should put a detailed description of the smell. Normally this will give further detail about the description you have chosen in the previous column.

TASTE

All these qualities should be graded 1–5.

There follows a further explanation of the taste categories.

Sweetness or the lack of it is the first sensation as the cider hits the tip of your tongue. Sweetness always needs to be balanced by acidity or it will be cloying.

1. Completely dry
2. Off-dry
3. Medium dry
4. Semi-sweet
5. Sweet

Acidity makes cider taste crisp. You notice its effect on the sides of your tongue. It must be balanced by sweetness, tannin and alcohol: a cider with too little of these and too much acidity will taste unpleasantly tart.

Tannin is the mouth-drying substance found in cider. It contributes to the body and weight of the cider. Tannin must be balanced by fruit flavour and acidity to produce a good rounded flavour.

Alcohol is your perception by taste of its alcohol content. You have already recorded its actual content on sheet 1.

Flavour description Put here a description of the flavour of the cider. That is usually done by comparison or analogy with the flavour of something else. You may use any and as many descriptions as you wish but there follows a series of suggested descriptions:

Flowery/fruity: Flowery, fruity, exotic fruits, cider apple, apple fruit, vanilla, dessert apple, culinary apple.

Qualities: Fresh, acid, bitter, astringent, sweet, texture (mouthfeel?).

Heavy flavours: Animal, woody, vat dregs, medicinal/chemical, underwood.

Heated flavours: Caramel, cooked apple, straw/hay, vegetal.

Fermented flavours: Butter, mushroom, yeast.

Weight or **body** describes the different impressions of weight and size the cider gives in the mouth. This is what is referred to by the terms full-, medium- and light-bodied.

Length is the final factor to consider when assessing a cider. A cider with good length has something to say to all parts of your palate and leaves a lingering taste in your mouth after you swallow it.

Balance is the relationship between all elements of the cider: sweetness, acidity, fruit, body, tannin and alcohol. An unbalanced cider will taste as though it is lacking something.

OVERALL

Insert the description which best describes the style of the cider. Do not use more than one description. Use the 'other' description sparingly.

CIDER STYLE

1. Crisp, fresh, light
2. Green, tangy, sharp
3. Intense, nutty
4. Ripe, toasty
5. Aromatic
6. Luscious, full
7. Other – specify

RATING

Please rate the cider 1–10 with 1 being awful and 10 superb.

COMMENTS/DESCRIPTION

Add any descriptions and comments of your own which you care to make. Try to give an overall impression of the cider.

TASTER'S NAME

Date of Tasting	Name of Cider	Date Fermentation Commenced	Region	Apples	Alcohol Content	Sparkling Y/N

TASTER'S NAME

Date of Tasting	Name of Cider	Colour						Nose				
		Limpidity	Brilliance	Intensity	Tint		Intensity	Aromatic Nuances (Category)		Aromatic Nuances (Description)
					No.	Description		No.	Description	

TASTER'S NAME

Date of Tasting	Name of Cider	Taste								Overall		
		Sweetness	Acidity	Tannin	Alcohol	Flavour Description	Body	Length	Balance	Cider Style	Rating	Comments

APPENDIX 5: FURTHER READING

CIDERMAKING METHOD

Lea, Andrew. *Craft Cidermaking* (2nd edition). The Good Life Press Limited, 2010.

Pooley, Michael and Lomax, John. *Real Cidermaking on a Small Scale*. Special Interest Model Books, 2002.

Proulx, Annie and Nichols, Lew. *Cider: Making, Using and Enjoying Sweet and Hard Cider* (3rd edition). Storey Publishing, 2003.

Watson, Ben. *Cider Hard and Sweet* (2nd edition). The Countryman Press, 2008.

ORCHARD MANAGEMENT

Baker, Harry. *Growing Fruit*. Octopus Publishing Group, 2006.

Hessayon, Dr D. G. *The Pest and Weed Expert*. Expert Books, 2008.

Phillips, Michael. *The Apple Grower*. Chelsea Green Publishing Company, 2005.

Rowe, Alan. *Success with Apples and Pears to Eat and Drink*. Groundnut Publishing, 2008.

Umpelby, Roger and Copas, Liz. *Growing Cider Apples: A Guide to Good Orchard Practice*. National Association of Cider Makers, 2002.

APPLE VARIETIES

Copas, Liz. *A Somersetshire Pomona: The Cider Apples of Somersetshire*. Dovecote Press, 2001.

Morgan, Joan and Richards, Alison. *The New Book of Apples: The Definitive Guide to Apples including over 2,000 Varieties* (2nd edition). Ebony Press, 2002.

HISTORY OF CIDERMAKING

Crowden, James. *Cider – The Forgotten Miracle*. Cyder Press 2, 1999.

Crowden, James. *Ciderland*. Birlinn Limited, 2008.

French, R.K. *The History and Virtues of Cyder*. Robert Hale Ltd, 2010.

Legg, Philippa. *Cidermaking in Somerset*. Somerset Rural Life Museum, 1984.

Legg, Philippa. *So Merry Let us Be: Living Traditions of Somerset Cider*. Somerset Books, 1986.

Quinion, Michael B. *Cidermaking*. Shire Publications Ltd, 1982.

OLDER WRITING

A Lover of Planting. *The Compleat Planter and Cyderist*. London, 1685.

Austen, Ralph. *Treatise of Fruit Trees and The Spiritual Use of an Orchard*. 1653 and 1657.

Beale, John. *Herefordshire Orchards: A Pattern for all England*. 1656.

Digby, Sir Kenelm. *The Closet Opened*. 1669; reprinted by Prospect Books, 1997.

Evelyn, John. *Sylva, A Pomona*, and *Aphorisms on Cider*. John Beale et al., Royal Society, 1664.

Haines, Sir Richard. *Aphorisms on the New Way of Improving Cider*. 1684.

Knight, Thomas. *A Treatise on the Culture of the Apple and Pear and the manufacture of Cider and Perry*. Proctor, Ludlow, 1808.

Phillips, John. *Cyder: a Poem*. H. Hills, Blackfriars, 1708.

Radcliffe Cooke, C. W. *A Book about Cider and Perry*. London, 1898.

Stafford, Hugh. *A Treatise on Cyder Making*. 1759.

Worlidge, John. *Vinetum Brittanicum or Treatise on Cider*. London, 1676.

GENERAL INTEREST

Bunker, Bob. *Farmhouse Cider and Scrumpy*. Bossiney Books, 1999.

Stone, Alan. *Somersetshire Cider Handbook*. Somersetshire History, 2009.

Various contributors, edited by Simon Hall and Katie Hunt. *Cider*. Campaign for Real Ale Ltd, 2009.

APPENDIX 6:
ADDITIONAL INFORMATION

CIDER FORA

Cider Workshop. This Google group is the leading cider forum. It is a mine
of useful cidermaking experience and information.
Website: www.ciderworkshop.com.

UKCider, another useful Google group. Website: www.ukcider.co.uk.

EQUIPMENT SUPPLIES

Art of Brewing, D8 Barwell Business Park, Leatherhead Road, Chessington,
Surrey KT9 2NY. Telephone: 020 8397 2111.
Website: www.art-of-brewing.co.uk.

Bottle Company (South) Ltd, Broadmead Lane, Keynsham, Bristol BS31 1ST.
Telephone: 0117 986 9667. Website: www.bottlecompanysouth.co.uk.

Brouwland, Korspelsesteenweg 86, 3581 Beverlo, Belgium.
Telephone: +32 011 40 14 08. Website: www.brouwland.com/en.

Fruit Shark (the UK distributor of an excellent Czech electric mill).
Telephone: 07837 030 860. Website: www.fruitshark.co.uk.

HomeBrewShop, 153 Lawsons Road, Thornton-Cleveleys, Lancashire FY5
4PL. Telephone: 01253 827793. Website: www.homebrewshop.co.uk.

Hop & Grape, 117 North Road, Darlington, Co. Durham DL1 2PS.
Telephone: 01325 380780. Website: www.hopandgrape.co.uk.

Laboratoires Standa (suppliers of KlerCidre), 68 rue Robert Kaskoreff,
14050 Caen Cedex 4, France. Telephone: +33 231 29 19 73.
Website: www.standa-fr.com.

Plastor (container suppliers), Smithfield Road, Woodlands Park,
Maidenhead, Berkshire SL6 3NP. Telephone: 01628 829800.
Website: www.plastor.co.uk.

The Home Brew Shop, 10 Alexandra Road, Farnborough, Hampshire GU14
6DA. Telephone: 01252 540 386.
Website: www.the-home-brew-shop.co.uk.

Vigo Ltd (the leading cider equipment supplier), Dunkeswell, Honiton,
Devonshire EX14 4LF. For larger producers – Telephone: 01404
890262. Website: www.vigoltd.com. For domestic producers –
Telephone: 01404 892101. Website: www.vigopresses.co.uk.

GENERAL INFORMATION

The CiderWorkshop. Website: www.ciderworkshop.com (an informative
website associated with the Cider Workshop Google group).

Dorset Cider. Website: www.dorsetcider.com.

Orchards Live, Castle Cottage, Blakeshill Road, Landkey, Barnstaple, Devonshire EX32 0LP. Website: www.orchardslive.org.uk.

Real Cider. Telephone: 07888 701588. Website: www.real-cider.co.uk.

Stonehelm Alcohol Calculator (useful online calculation facility). Website: www.stonehelm.co.uk.

Wine Adds (additive calculator). Website: www.wineadds.com.

Wittenham Hill Cider Portal (Andrew Lea's website – a mine of information). Website: www.cider.org.uk.

UK Cider (an informative website associated with the UKCider Google group). Website: www.ukcider.co.uk.

TREE SUPPLIERS

Bernwode Fruit Trees, Kingswood Lane, Ludgershall, Buckinghamshire HP18 9RB. Telephone: 01844 237415.
Website: www.bernwodefruittrees.co.uk.

Brogdale National Fruit Collection, Brogdale Road, Faversham, Kent ME13 8XZ. Telephone: 01795 536250. Website: www.brogdale.org.

Cider Apple Trees, Kerian, Corkscrew Lane, Woolston, Nr North Cadbury, Somersetshire BA22 7BP. Telephone: 01963 441101.
Website: www.ciderappletrees.co.uk.

H. P. Bulmer plc, Plough Lane, Herefordshire HR4 0LE.
Telephone: 01432 352000.

Keepers Nursery, Gallants Court, East Farleigh, Maidstone, Kent ME15 0LE. Telephone: 01622 726465. Website: www.fruittree.co.uk.

Lodge Farm Trees, Lodge Farm, Rockhampton, Berkeley, Gloucestershire GL13 9DY. Telephone: 01454 260310.
Website: www.lodgefarmtrees.co.uk.

Thornhayes Nursery Ltd, St Andrews Wood, Dulford, Cullompton, Devonshire EX15 2DF. Telephone: 01884 266746.
Website: www.thornhayes-nursery.co.uk.

APPLE INFORMATION

Brogdale National Fruit Collection, Brogdale Road, Faversham, Kent ME13 8XZ. Telephone: 01795 536250.
Website: www.brogdalecollections.co.uk.

Common Ground, Gold Hill House, 21 High Street, Shaftesbury, Dorsetshire SP7 8JE. Telephone: 01747 850820.
Website: www.commonground.org.uk; www.england-in-particular.info.

Marcher Apple Network, Hopesay, Craven Arms, Shropshire SY7 8HD.
Website: www.marcherapple.net.

The Big Apple Association. Website: www.bigapple.org.uk.

CIDER COMPETITIONS

Frome Cheese Show, The Show Office, Rodden Road, Frome, Somersetshire
BA11 2AH. Telephone: 01373 463600.
Website: www.fromecheeseshow.co.uk.

Mid-Somerset Show, Rowberrow Farm, Plummers Lane, Priddy, Wells,
Somersetshire BA5 3DA. Telephone: 01749 870124.
Website: www.midSomersetshow.org.uk.

Putley Cider and Perry Trials.
Website: www.bigapple.org.uk/cider_perry_trials.

Royal Bath and West Show, The Showground, Shepton Mallet, Somersetshire
BA4 6QN. Telephone: 01749 822200.
Website: www.bathandwest.com.

The Three Counties Show, The Malvern Showground, Worcestershire WR13
6NW. Telephone: 01684 584900. Website: www.threecounties.co.uk.

MUSEUMS

Somerset Rural Life Museum, Abbey Farm, Chilkwell Street, Glastonbury,
Somersetshire BA6 8DB. Telephone: 01458 831197.
Website: www.Somerset.gov.uk/archives/museums/Intro.htm.

The Cider Museum Hereford, 21 Ryelands Street, Hereford, Herefordshire
HR4 0LW. Telephone: 01432 354207.
Website: www.cidermuseum.co.uk.

TRAINING COURSES

Cider Academy (Mitchell F&D Limited), 74 Holloway, Pershore,
Worcestershire WR10 1HP. Telephone: 01386 552324.
Website: www.cider-academy.co.uk.

COMMERCIAL CRAFT CIDER PRODUCERS

This list is deliberately idiosyncratic and by no means comprehensive.

146 Cider (a cider made in Hampshire and sold in local pubs and at
festivals). Website: www.146cider.blogspot.com.
Email: cider146@btinternet.com.

Ashridge Cider, Barkingdon Farm, Staverton, Totnes, Devonshire TQ9 6AN.
Telephone: 01364 654749 or 07919 992934.
Website: www.ashridgecider.co.uk.

Aspalls Cyder (available in supermarkets, pubs, bars and restaurants), The
Cyder House, Aspall Hall, Debenham, Suffolk IP14 6PD.
Telephone: 01728 860510. Website: www.aspall.co.uk.

Cider by Rosie (a cider made in Dorsetshire, sold in local pubs and
restaurants). Telephone: 01258 880543.
Website: www.ciderbyrosie.co.uk (no sales direct to the public).

Ciderniks (sold in local pubs, restaurants and other outlets), Kintbury, West Berkshire. Telephone: 07885 296789. Website: www.ciderniks.com.

Ciderpunk.com (specialist sellers of 'farmhouse ciders'), c/o Room 5, St Werbughs Community Centre, Horley Road, Bristol BS2 9TJ. Telephone: 0117 325 0067 (ask to be put through to Richard Higgs). Website: www.ciderpunk.com.

Hecks Farmhouse Cider (farm shop and many local shops), 9–11 Middle Leigh, Street, Somersetshire BA16 0LB. Telephone: 01458 442367. Website: www.hecksfarmhousecider.co.uk.

Henney's Cider Co Ltd (sold in supermarkets – no farm visits). Les Blanquettes, Bishops Frome, Herefordshire WR6 5BY. Website: www.henneys.co.uk.

Lambourn Valley Cider Company (sold at shows and festivals), The Malt House, Great Shefford, Hungerford, Berkshire RG17 7ED. Telephone: 01488 648441. Website: www.lambournvalleycider.co.uk.

New Forest Cider (farm shop and Borough Market), Littlemead, Pound Lane, Burley, Hampshire BH24 4ED. Telephone: 01425 403589. Website: www.newforestcider.co.uk.

Olivers Cider and Perry (farm shop and local pubs), The Old Hop Kilns, Moorhouse Farm, Ocle Pychard, Herefordshire HR1 3QZ. Telephone: 01432 820569. Website: www.theolivers.org.uk.

Orchard Pig (online shops and stores), West Bradley Orchard, West Bradley, Glastonbury, Somersetshire BA6 8LT. Telephone: 01458 851222. Website: www.orchardpig.co.uk.

Producers in Somerset – a useful list of Somersetshire cider producers. Website: www.ukcider.co.uk/wiki/index.php/Producers_in_Somerset

Quality English Cider (sold at Bath Farmers' Market), K. G. Consultants, The Bailiffs Cottage, The Green, Compton Dando, Pensford, Bristol BS39 4LE. Telephone: 01761 490624.

Rich's Cider Farm (farm shop, online shop, various pubs, etc.), Watchfield, Highbridge, Somersetshire TA9 4RD. Telephone: 01278 783681. Website: www.richscider.co.uk.

Rockingham Forest Cider (various local pubs listed on their website). Website: www.rockinghamforestcider.moonfruit.com.

Sheppy's Cider (farm shop, online shop, pubs and supermarkets), Three Bridges, Bradford-on-Tone, Taunton, Somersetshire TA4 1ER. Telephone: 01823 461233. Website: www.sheppyscider.com.

Somerset Cider Brandy & Burrow Hill Cider (the main licensed cider brandy producer in Britain also makes excellent cider, including outstanding 'English Method' sparkling cider; available in farm shop, online shop, pubs, restaurants and supermarkets), Pass Vale Farm, Burrow Hill,

Kingsbury Episcopi, Martock, Somersetshire TA12 6BU.
Telephone: 01460 240782. Website: www.ciderbrandy.co.uk.
Wilkins Farmhouse Cider (farm gate sales only – a West Country institution),
Land's End Farm, Mudgley, Wedmore, Somersetshire BS28 4TU.
Telephone: 01934 712385.

CIDER ASSOCIATIONS

National Association of Cidermakers (NACM), 6 Catherine Street, London
WC2B 5JJ. Website: www.cideruk.com.
South West Cidermakers Association, contact via NACM, 6 Catherine Street,
London, WC2B 5JJ. Website: www.cideruk.com
The Three Counties Cider and Perry Association.
Website: www.thethreecountiesciderandperryassociation.co.uk.
Welsh Cider and Perry Association. Website: www.welshcider.co.uk.

INDEX